THE MAKER'S INSTRUCTIONS

THE MAKER'S INSTRUCTIONS

A new look at the Ten Commandments

David Pawson

Anchor Recordings

**First published in 2013
by Anchor Recordings Ltd
72 The Street, Kennington, Ashford TN24 9HS UK**

**For more of David Pawson's teaching,
including MP3s, DVDs and CDs –**

www.davidpawson.com

For further information, email info@davidpawsonministry.com

ISBN 978 0 9575290 6 9

Printed by Createspace and
Printed in Great Britain by Imprint Digital, Exeter

Contents

This book is based on a series of talks. Originating as it does from the spoken word, its style will be found by many readers to be somewhat different from my usual written style. It is hoped that this will not detract from the substance of the biblical teaching found here.

As always, I ask the reader to compare everything I say or write with what is written in the Bible and, if at any point a conflict is found, always to rely upon the clear teaching of scripture.

David Pawson

INTRODUCTION

Then God issued this edict:

"I am Yahweh your God who liberated you from slavery in Egypt. You may worship no other God than me. You shall not make yourselves any idols; any images resembling animals, birds, or fish. You must never bow to an image or worship it in any way for I the Lord your God am very possessive. I will not share your affection with any other God. When I punish people for their sins, the punishment continues upon the children, grandchildren, and great-grandchildren of those who hate me. But I lavish my love upon thousands of those who love me and obey my commandments. You shall not use the name of Yahweh your God irreverently nor use it to swear to a falsehood. You will not escape punishment if you do. Remember to observe the Sabbath as a holy day. Six days a week are for your daily duties and your regular work but the seventh day is a day of Sabbath rest before the Lord your God. On that day you are to do no work of any kind, nor shall your son, daughter, or slaves whether men or women, or your cattle or your house guests. For in six days the Lord made the heaven and earth and sea and everything in them, and rested the seventh day. So he blessed the Sabbath day and set it aside for rest. Honour your father and mother that you may have a long, good life in the land the Lord your God will give you. You must not murder. You must not commit adultery. You must not steal. You must not lie. You must not be envious of your neighbour's house or want to sleep with his wife or want to own his slaves, oxen, donkeys, or anything else he has."

All the people saw the lightning and the smoke billowing from the mountain and heard the thunder and the long, frightening trumpet blast, and they stood at a distance, shaking with fear. They said to Moses, "You tell us what God says and we will obey, but don't let God speak directly to us or it will kill us."

"Don't be afraid," Moses told them, "for God has come in this way to show you his awesome power, so that from now on you will be afraid to sin against him." As the people stood in the distance, Moses entered into the deep darkness where God was, and the Lord told Moses to be his spokesman to the people of Israel. "You are witnesses to the fact that I have made known my will to you from heaven."

Exodus 20:1–22

That was a deep, solemn experience. God gave them just ten commandments to keep. There is a church where I went to be the minister many years ago, where I think I was primarily remembered for one thing: I was the minister who 'abolished the Ten Commandments'. There was a plaster, gothic-print panel behind the pulpit, and painted on it in chocolate brown paint were the Ten Commandments. Nobody could remember when they first appeared, though quite a lot of members could remember how often they had been varnished when the rest of the church had been decorated. Whenever I preached, I knew they were reading, behind me: "Thou shalt not...." So during that year the painted board went. The minister who abolished the Ten Commandments! Of course, I didn't mean to do so.

Christ said, "I came not to abolish but to fulfil...." One of the widely held misunderstandings is that Christians have nothing to do with the Ten Commandments. I remember seeing a cartoon in *Punch* magazine—it showed a rather disconsolate vicar standing at the door of his church against the notice board which announced a series of sermons on the Ten Commandments. Through the open door, you could see empty pews behind the vicar and he was looking very wistfully across to the cinema where there was a great hoarding which read: '*Stupendous, sensational, The Ten Commandments*' and there was a queue of people from the cinema door right around the corner.

The vicar was looking rather wistfully over the crowds. However, the people who went to see that film were not seeking *sanctification* but *sensation.* They were seeking entertainment not edification, and although the film was entitled *The Ten Commandments* they played a very minor part in the film. For the most part it was a typical Hollywood extravaganza, though Cecil B. DeMille himself appeared at the beginning of the film and said briefly that in his personal view he believed that Western civilisation had been built on the Ten Commandments, and there is an element of truth in that.

I have twenty-one points to make, which can be divided up into three main points.

I want to give you seven reasons why people don't study the Ten Commandments and don't think I ought to take you through them.

I want to give you seven reasons why I'm going to take you through the Ten Commandments and why I believe you ought to.

Then I'm going to give you seven features of the Ten Commandments that will start you thinking.

To many people it's a very strange thing to do nowadays – to go way back to the Ten Commandments.

Here are the seven reasons that I have come across why people say you shouldn't bother with the Ten Commandments today. Firstly, they are rules and regulations. Man doesn't need rules now, he has grown up and come of age. In this sophisticated, scientific era we don't need to be told how to behave. Treat us as mature adults, we are not kids any more. We don't need to be told how to behave. Assume people have common sense.

Now this is being said on many sides in the name of 'freedom'. What people need is liberty, to be treated as able to discipline themselves. This cry is being heard in many areas. Well, it would be very nice if that could be so but it doesn't work.

When people say, "Leave it to common sense", I'm afraid sense isn't all that common. We have found that in practice, in almost every sphere of life, we have got to have rules or we just cannot live together. If I get into my car, I have to recognise that if everybody did as they liked on the roads it would be absolutely impossible to drive. If I go and play football I have to recognise that if there are going to be no rules it will be impossible to play the game. That is what's wrong with the game of rounders as far as I understand:

every time I play it there is a new set of rules. Every sphere of life has shown that people cannot behave well together in society without rules. There have to be some limits to our liberty if we are to enjoy that liberty, and the Ten Commandments tell us that also. But someone says, "Who has a right to tell me what to do? No man has the right to go to another and tell him how to behave." But God has the right to make rules for my life! He has the authority to tell me how to behave – because he made me – and he can also delegate that authority to others.

The second objection I come across is that the Ten Commandments are too negative, full of 'thou shalt not'. Of course, they are not all like that. Some of them are quite positive: six days shalt thou labour. That's positive – I wouldn't think it is any more popular for being so – but they are on the whole negative. People say this is bad psychology. If you really want to get a good response from people, don't go with a list of 'nots' – that will have just the opposite effect to the one you desire; it will set up repression; it will make them want what is forbidden. But I prefer God to psychology if this is what psychology says. I think God knows better. I believe God knows that if you are going to have any morality at all you not only have to define what is right, you also have to define what is wrong. Otherwise people will not understand the limits of morality. You have to say, "This is right and this is wrong," and then people know where they are. We need negatives. Even before he fell, Adam in the Garden of Eden needed a negative to make voluntary choice possible. If God had not put a tree in the Garden of Eden and told Adam that he couldn't eat of that tree, Adam would not have had a voluntary choice of choosing God's way.

Furthermore, since the Fall it has been necessary for God to add to the list of 'thou shalt nots' because, having made a free choice and chosen the wrong one, there are many other things that man goes on to do which God must clearly say are wrong.

Thirdly, there are those who object to absolute morality and want it all to be relative. I mean by that they want a morality that can be changed and adapted to circumstances. The objection is that these Ten Commandments lay down absolutes, which are always right or always wrong in every situation. There are many voices today being heard to say, "That is not true morality – morals will change in different situations, they are relative, not absolute. They can't always be this way, you've got to adapt." Now I honestly believe that once you lose absolutes in morals you lose morals. Sooner or later, if a thing is *sometimes* right or wrong, you get to the point where you do not know the difference between right and wrong. There have to be some absolutes, even if there are some questions that do change with circumstances.

A fourth objection is that the Ten Commandments are old-fashioned and so out of date. After all, they were produced some 3,500 years ago. How can rules produced in a society and a nation so far removed from ours, and in circumstances so different, possibly be relevant to me today? They are simply obsolete. There was a Dr. Vine (a medical doctor) in Yorkshire who spoke to a youth club when he was in his nineties. A girl at the end said, "Doctor Vine, you're old fashioned in your views."

He replied, "My dear young lady, you came into the world in an old-fashioned way and you'll go out of it in an old-fashioned way," which was a very good answer to that modern Miss!

The simple truth is that though our circumstances have changed, our clothes and fashions have changed and our technology has changed, human nature has not changed, and neither has divine nature. God and men are still the same. Read the Ten Commandments and then go out and read the news, and then tell me these commandments are old-fashioned and that they no longer fit our society! They are about the very things that human beings struggle with today. The newspaper headlines say nothing new at all, it's all there. Our problems of relationships either with each other or with him have not changed, so the Commandments are not old-fashioned.

Fifthly: "The Ten Commandments belong to the Jews and we are Christians; we have enough teaching in the New Testament from Christ without the Ten Commandments. That's Jewish, that's going back to the Old Testament. We live in the New Testament." Now this is a rather more subtle point. Let me remind you that Jesus was a Jew and that he was born under the Law, under the Ten Commandments. Let me remind you that nine out of the Ten (the exception is significant and we'll discuss that later) are repeated in the New Testament verbatim and they apply to Christians as well. Let me remind you that Jesus said, "Not one jot or tittle of the law will pass away," and that he came to fulfil it, to get it translated from legislation into action, to get it done *fully* – he didn't come to abolish or destroy the law.

Then there are those who say, in a more subtle way, that the Ten Commandments should not be studied by Christians because we are under grace and not under law, and that is a very compelling argument. I agree that we are not under law, the New Testament says we are not. But what does that phrase mean? Is it that we don't need to bother about the will of God now? That we don't need to study his commands? Far from it, that phrase is concerned primarily with the basis of our relationship to God. If you read the context, it is saying very clearly that you cannot establish your relationship with God by keeping the Ten Commandments. To do that would put you under the law; it would put you under the curse of it because you can't keep them. To live under the law, to have the Ten Commandments hanging as a threat over your head, is something Christians have left far behind. We are not under law in the sense of having to keep the commandments to be right with God. The grace of God has produced a completely new basis for our relationship with him.

We are not under law, we are under grace. But in another sense we are committed to the law of God. More about that below, but the motive for keeping the law has changed totally. The motive under the old law was to get right with God and to earn the right, the righteousness, to enter heaven – and it failed miserably because no one could do it. The new motive for keeping God's law is gratitude. Jesus said, "If you love me you'll keep my commandments," and since he repeated the Ten Commandments it follows that he includes them as an expression of our love. In other words, I no longer keep the Ten Commandments in order to get to heaven but because I hope to go there. That makes the law my servant and not my master. I am no longer under it.

The last argument against studying the Ten Commandments is this: that love is all that's needed. I'm going to call it love-ism. There are many professing Christians (as well as others) saying that the only commandment we need is love – that if we love our neighbour and love God then we can forget the Ten Commandments. It sounds at first sight like a thoroughly biblical position, for the New Testament says, "Love is the fulfilling of the law", and what does, "thou shalt not kill", "thou shalt not steal", "thou shalt not commit adultery" mean but, "love your neighbour"? Yet there is a dreadful flaw in this. If that is all I need to be told – to love – then I don't need any of the other teaching of the New Testament.

But, in the name of love, people have begun to advocate breaking the commandments. People who say that only love is needed are beginning to say that murder can be justified if you do it out of love. Adultery can be justified if you do it out of love. Stealing can be justified if you do it out of love. Lying can be justified if you do it out of love. Maybe you are wondering at the moment how you could think you are loving someone yet do these things. Well let me tell you.

Here's a loved one dying in dreadful pain and just cannot cope with it, and the loved one is pleading with you to give them some pills. The new morality says: as long as you love them, give them the pills, kill them. There are those who are arguing that it is far better today for a husband and wife who cannot get on with each other, who make their lives and their children's lives a misery, and know someone else with whom they could make a happy marriage, because there is love, to go and commit adultery.

What about a mother who steals a loaf of bread for a starving child because she loves that child? See what I'm saying—that if you say that love is the only rule, you are liable to start breaking the other laws. Does that matter? Yes, it does. God's definition of love is a love that keeps the commandments, not that breaks them. Because our understanding and our wisdom are limited and finite, I need to be told how to love. I need to be told what love will do. I dare not trust my own feelings in this. Let me give you a simple illustration. Two young people fall in love, they want to be married. They come to ask me when they can fix the date. They get a surprise. I talk to them about marriage, recommend books to them, tell them how to prepare for the relationship, and they might well say, "You don't understand, pastor, we don't need to be told how to be married. Everything's going to be fine. We love each other. That's all that's needed."

If that were all that is needed, why do so many marriages break down? It is *not* all that is needed, though there can sometimes be confusion about how it should be expressed. So there is need for help and guidance, as every marriage guidance bureau would tell you. So God knows that you love him and each other, but that's not enough. He wants to guide that love. He wants to tell you what love will do. With his wisdom and infinite knowledge of the situation he knows how best love can express itself and so he has given you commandments to show you how that love can reach out. I think the real reason why people don't like studying the Ten Commandments is very simple. J. B. Phillips translated one word in the letter to the Romans like this: "It is the straight edge of God's law that shows us how crooked we are." Remember that sentence. It brings me to the first of the seven reasons why we do study the Ten Commandments, and why it is a help to do so. First, it helps you to define sin. What does that little word mean? How do I know if I've got the disease? How do I know if I am a sinner? One very simple way to find out is to use *the straight edge of God's law*. How do you know if a wall is crooked? By just putting a straight edge against it. How do you know if a man is crooked? By just putting the law of God against him. Thank God for the law.

Do you know that the Ten Commandments have brought many people to Christ? Billy Graham, when preaching, often went through the Ten Commandments? Why? Because he knew that until people feel crooked, they don't want to get straightened. He knew that until people realise they have the dreadful killer disease of sin they won't seek a cure in Christ. So he shows them the straight edge of God's law. It defines sin. Sin is not what the Sunday newspapers call sin. It's not what the film advertisements call sin. Sin is what *God* calls sin, and it is a transgression of the law. Therefore, if you want to know if you have got the disease of sin, just sit down and read through the Ten Commandments and tick those you have kept and put a cross against those you have broken—that will tell you. This defines sin, it diagnoses our disease.

Even after I have come to Christ I still have problems with sin. There is my old self – what the Bible calls the "flesh" – still hanging around. I need to know if I am going to grow; I need to know what areas in my life still are being contaminated by sin. How will I know that? By studying the straight edge of God's law.

So whether I am an unbeliever or a believer, it defines sin for me. Secondly, it helps me to receive guidance. I hope this won't shock you, but a man came to me and he told me to my face that he felt led by God to leave his wife and go and live with another woman. He told me so sincerely that he prayed about it, that he had thought about it, and that he was convinced God was telling him to do this. I was convinced straightaway that God was not saying this, because God does not contradict himself.

There are two sorts of guidance we need – general and particular. The *general* guidance into the will of God applies to every person in every situation – to the whole of life. The *particular* guidance is the will of God for me in these circumstances in this place. The Ten Commandments are concerned with *general* guidance. I believe that some people have difficulty getting particular guidance because they are ignoring general guidance. In other words, if we are not already in line with the *known* will of God, we are not likely to get an answer to the *unknown* question of his will. What right have I to ask him for particular guidance for me in a situation if I am ignoring all that he has already told me to do?

So the general guidance helps us to receive guidance, on the basis of which God is then prepared to guide us particularly. Here is an illustration: I think God is far more interested in how we do our work than in what work we do. Yet I have had scores of young people come to me asking about this question of guidance regarding their work, and their concern with what they should do. Should I be a missionary? Should I be a butcher? Should I be a lawyer? What should I be? I want to say, "Look, God is far more interested in you being a good lawyer and a good butcher and a good missionary." The general guidance of God in the Bible is this: do your work to God's glory. If a person is not doing their existing work already to Christ, whatever that work is, why should they expect God to tell them what job he wants them to do? The order is: general guidance of the will of God first, the particular guidance second, and the Ten Commandments are the general guidance.

Thirdly, it helps us to understand the character of God. Someone who reads the Ten Commandments might say, "Well he's a killjoy for a start. He's a kind of God who as soon as you enjoy yourselves says, 'Thou shalt not.'"

It is rather like the little boy who went to school and was asked, "What's your name?" He said, "My name is Johnny Don't." That was what his mother always called him. The feeling is that the Ten Commandments show you the kind of God who sits up in heaven and says, "Someone's enjoying themselves on earth. Send a commandment straightaway." Nothing could be further from the truth. I'll tell you what sort of a God the Ten Commandments reveal: a God who has got very high standards for a start, and who wants the best for people, a God who doesn't try and spoil your fun but who says, "You do that and it will spoil your fun." He is a God who says, "If you want to enjoy life, I made it and here are my instructions for its use."

If you want to get the best out of your life and your society, this is how it is to be run. It is God who wants the best who is revealed in the Ten Commandments—a God who is not content with anything less. So the Ten Commandments help us to understand something important about God.

Fourthly, the Ten Commandments help us to avoid suffering. There are two ways of gaining knowledge of evil. One is to listen to someone else, and the other is to do it yourself. There is a tragic effect of knowing evil at first hand rather than secondhand. Thank God if you know evil secondhand. It will save you a lot of suffering. That was the problem of the tree of knowledge of good and evil in the Garden of Eden. God did not want Adam to touch it because he did not want him to have first-hand knowledge of evil. He wanted him to take his word for it – that there is evil – and leave it there.

Let me give you a down-to-earth illustration. Here is a young girl who is chaste and she enjoys innocence. But she is a modern girl and says, "I'm not going to listen to my parents who say that chastity is right and unchastity is wrong. I'm going to find out for myself. I'm going to experience these things and come to my own conclusion."

She will discover that unchastity is wrong but she will discover it the hard way because one of the effects will be that she will no longer be able to enjoy innocence. Her knowledge of evil will be first hand, but her knowledge of good will have become secondhand. She can't go back to the innocence. She can be forgiven but she can't go back to innocence – and that is a different thing. God does not want you to experience evil at first-hand. He does not want you to face the suffering. He wants you to have second-hand knowledge of evil and first hand knowledge of good. The Ten Commandments stand there to prevent people from having first-hand knowledge of evil with the loss of innocence, which they can never again enjoy once they have broken them.

Fifthly, study of the Ten Commandments helps us to lift the level of our community life. The one thing our nation needs desperately is law-abiding citizens, not just those who abide by human laws but those who abide by divine laws. Our community is perishing for lack of people who recognise certain standards and guidelines. Jesus taught that if you really act according to the guidelines, you will act as salt in the earth. He meant, therefore, acting as a fertiliser and a disinfectant. These are the two uses of salt, which he had in mind as he explained: a fertiliser to promote the growth of what is good and a disinfectant to limit the spread of evil. He taught: you can be salt. He said it just before he talked in the Sermon on the Mount about not abolishing the law but fulfilling it. If there were more people in our community who recognised the Ten Commandments, our social life would be transformed in this country.

Sixthly, the study of the Ten Commandments will help you to guide your children. Let me paint for you two extremes. Let us say there are two teenagers from different families. In the one home everything is laid down the line. The mother and father are always making rules. So the father and mother have it all laid down. The poor teenager is always having to come and go at the right time and all the rest of it. There is a repression in that home, and the teenager says (and I have heard a girl say this to her mother), "Just you wait until I'm old enough to get out of this house. I'm going to have a flat of my own and get rid of you. I'm going to go away."

That kind of repressive home that's nothing but rules and regulations has a damaging effect on children. But at the other extreme, here's another teenager – her parents don't care when she comes in. There are no rules. "Here's the door key: get yourself some fish and chips, it's all free." The interesting thing psychologists have discovered is that this second teenager will feel dreadfully insecure, that it will do harm to them, that in fact the freedom to do whatever they wish as children is in fact not the right thing and will lead them to a deep insecurity. Funnily enough, teenagers appreciate it deeply when parents have reasonable rules. It gives them a security because they know the limits within which they are free – and you damage a child on the one hand by having nothing but rules and regulations, and on the other hand by having none. The security that comes into a Christian home where the parents are under the same rules as the children gives a child that guideline, that instinctive conscience, that is going to help him or her all through life to feel that there is some security.

That does not mean that a child accepts all the guidelines as interpreted by the parent. When a child grows up he has to ask himself: were my parents right in saying that was wrong? I myself have come to certain conclusions that are different from the moral judgments of my parents, but that is not an argument about the Ten Commandments. I knew that my parents recognised those just as much as I need to and that we are all under certain clear guidelines.

Seven, the Ten Commandments help us to please Jesus. Don't you want to do that if you're a Christian? Don't you want to please him? Then the answer is very simple. Jesus said, "If you love me, keep my commandments. That's how you'll please me. That's how you'll show that you really love me." Jesus came to get the law done. He didn't come to get rid of it. He came to help people to do it. Nothing pleases the Lord more than those who show their love by keeping his commandments. You are saying to the Lord Jesus, "I love you so much that your wish is my command."

Now we move to the third and last main introductory point by way of introduction: seven features of the Ten Commandments just to get you thinking. Though there are some 630 commandments in the Old Testament (and over 1100 imperatives in the New), *these* commandments number just ten. Is that a coincidence? Ten fingers. Little Jewish children were taught to memorise them on their fingers. God put them so simply that any of us can memorise them, and on two hands you have five commandments relating us to God and five relating us to other people—very simple. The fifth one, incidentally – "Honour your father and mother" – is really a commandment relating you rightly to God, because until you are a mature person your mother and father are God's delegated authorities to you. In honouring them you are honouring him. I hope that you could recite all of the Ten Commandments straight through. If not, why not learn them now?

Secondly, notice that God comes first. One of the commonest ideas that I have to try and correct all the time is the idea has got around that if you keep the second five you don't need to bother with the first five. Have you come across this? Love your neighbour and be kind to them and keep that lot, and God excuses you the first five. Any student need only tackle five out of ten — you know the kind of thing. There is the idea that as long as we love our neighbour that is all that God requires. Jesus said, "The first commandment is to love God," putting all the five into one. He said, "The second commandment is to love your neighbour as yourself," putting all five into one. But you notice which he said is the first. Before you start thinking about getting right with your neighbour, the Ten Commandments lead to the matter: How about God? Are you loving God first? Are you keeping his commandments? – So God first.

Third, the commandments are all addressed to a single individual — you. The word "you" is in the singular. They are not addressed to communities. They are not addressed to groups of people. They are not addressed to nations. They are addressed to you sitting where you do in a pew as if you were the only person in the building. "You shall not," meaning that every person is responsible to God only for one person — himself or herself. God deals with us as individuals and he doesn't say, "Britain is breaking my laws." He says, "You are."

In these days it is only too easy to believe in what I would call collective evil. You know, "Isn't the nation in a sad state? Isn't the world in a dreadful mess and aren't those people dreadful who throw bombs?" It is so easy to say "them", but God says *you*, by yourself. I'm only going to hold *you* responsible for obeying my laws. We stand alone before God to answer as to whether we have kept his laws.

Four — the ten commandments cover deed, word, and thought. They're not just concerned with the part that shows. A little boy is sent by his mother to wash his hands before a meal, then he returns. "Let's see, have you washed?"

"Yes."

"Turn them over. Back upstairs...."

At an adult level we behave like little children. We try to get the part that shows right, but we are not so bothered by the part that doesn't show. But God's commandments are concerned not just with outward deeds like killing and adultery, but with words – "Thou shalt not bear false witness", and with thoughts: "Thou shalt not covet". They are concerned with what you are like on the *inside* as well as the outside, what you do, say and think – your whole personality. That is why Jesus taught that you can murder with a word and commit adultery with a thought. We are not just to say, "Have I kept this commandment in deed?" but, "Have I kept it in word and in thought?" Then you are reading a commandment properly.

Fifthly, the commandments are ten but they are in fact one. Together they are a unit, like a perfect pearl necklace with ten pearls of God's wisdom. They are a unity and therefore the Bible says quite clearly that if you break them at any point, you have broken the whole law. (See the Epistle of James, chapter 2.)

If my wife has a necklace and the thread snaps at only one point, do you know what she says to me? She does not say, "The thread has broken at one point." She says, "I've broken my necklace." Do you understand that? Think of a chain that has a lot of links that's doing a job – pulling a car, or lifting a weight – one link gone, and it's broken; the whole thing has gone.

It is so important to realise the Ten Commandments are one whole. There is no such thing as 'six out of ten' pass mark. Break one and you have broken the lot. They give a picture of God's will for your life, and if you break it at any point you have spoiled the pattern.

Sixthly, the thread that ties together all these ten pearls can be summed up in one word: respect. Respect God – respect his position (no others gods besides him); respect his character—no image like his personality. Respect his name. Respect his day. Respect his representatives—your mother and father.

Then when you move to the second part: respect your neighbour's life; respect his marriage; respect his property; respect his reputation. Is not respect one of the most rare qualities in our society – with satire and comedy about anybody and everybody; society that enjoys taking people apart and making them objects of ridicule. God tells us to respect him and to respect each other.

Finally, observe that God addressed the Ten Commandments to those who had been saved. He says, "I am the Lord your God." His words mean: I am only speaking to you like this because of what I have done for you; I brought you out of slavery in Egypt and it is because of that I have a right to say this is how I want you to respond; this is how I want you to live now; I have given you your freedom but these are the limits to that freedom.

God's will is for those who have been redeemed and saved primarily. I believe these Ten Commandments are for those who have been brought out of slavery into freedom by God. Did you realise that every one of the Ten Commandments carried the death penalty? Did you realise that is how seriously God takes his commandments?

I used to think this was unfair. "God you've got it all out of proportion. For any of these you would put a man to death?" God's answer would be: Yes, do you know why? Because I want my universe right – I want it perfect – and if you have broken even one, you have spoiled my universe. I can't let you live forever in it. You'd go on spoiling it forever.

It is a solemn thought that I stand before God as a lawbreaker who deserves the penalty of death. I don't deserve to live in God's universe forever. God has told me I can't if I break his laws. Is there no way through? Well there was one man, only one, who once lived two thousand years ago and he came and he kept every one of the Ten Commandments every day of his life for thirty-three years. Then he paid the death penalty for me—that's Jesus.

If I didn't know Jesus I would be frightened stiff by the Ten Commandments. Wouldn't you? The people who heard them originally were, and their response was: Moses, get us away from here quickly – you tell us what God says but God is getting too near us. That was how they felt but, when Jesus came, people didn't feel that way. Why not? Because he came to get the law done and he had a new way of getting it done – not to frighten people to death but to die for them, to give them such a love that they would *want* to keep the commandments.

God, we thank you that you didn't just create us and leave us to find out how to live, but that you kept in touch and that you told us what was right and what was wrong. We thank you for the security this gives us as your children. Lord, we pray that before we start asking you for guidance about the things we are unsure about, we may be earnest to do what we are sure about. We love you and we want to obey you. *Amen*

> *"Trust and obey for there's no other way*
> *to be happy in Jesus but to trust and obey."*

1

NO OTHER GODS

While Paul was waiting for them in Athens, he was deeply troubled by all the idols he saw everywhere throughout the city. He went to the synagogue for discussions with the Jews and the devout Gentiles and spoke daily in the public square to all who happened to be there. He also had an encounter with some of the Epicurean and Stoic philosophers. Their reaction when he told them about Jesus and his resurrection was, "He's a dreamer," or, "He's pushing some foreign religion."

But they invited him to the forum at Mars Hill. "Come and tell us more about this new religion," they said, "for you are saying rather startling things and we want to hear more." I should explain that all the Athenians as well as the foreigners in Athens seemed to spend all their time discussing their latest new ideas.

So Paul, standing before them at the Mars Hill forum, addressed them as follows: "Men of Athens I noticed that you are very religious, for as I was out walking I saw your many altars and one of them had this inscription on it: 'To the unknown God'. You have been worshipping him without knowing who he is, and now I wish to tell you about him. He made the world and everything in it, and since he is Lord of heaven and earth, he doesn't live in man-made temples, and human hands can't minister to his needs for he has no needs. He himself gives life and breath to everything and satisfies every need there is. He created all the people of the world from one man, Adam, and scattered the nations across the face of the earth. He decided beforehand which should rise and fall and when. He determined their boundaries. His purpose in all this is that they should seek after God, and perhaps feel their way toward him and find him, though he is not far from any one of us. For in him we live and move, and as one of your own poets says, 'We are the sons of God.' If this is true we shouldn't think of God as an idol made by men from gold or silver, or chipped from stone. God tolerated man's past ignorance about these things but now he commands everyone to put away idols and worship only him. For he has set a day for justly judging the world by the man whom he has appointed, and has pointed him out by bringing him back to life again. When they heard Paul speak of the resurrection of a person who had been dead, some laughed, but others said, "We want to hear more about this later." That ended Paul's discussion with them but a few joined him and became believers. Among them was Dionysius, a member of the city council, and a woman named Damaris, and others.

Acts 17:16–34

The first commandment is: "I am Yahweh your God who liberated you from your slavery in Egypt. You may worship no other God than me." Not quite the form that you may know well, but another translation. Everybody has to have a god—that's the way we are made. Somebody said, "If there weren't a God we'd have to invent one." Huxley said that every man and woman has a god-shaped blank in their soul that feels empty and hollow – and human nature, like nature, abhors a vacuum, and wants to fill it with something or someone.

Someone has got to be the centre of your life. Someone or something has got to draw your affection and your devotion. You need to put your trust in someone or something to give your life meaning and value and purpose, and to see you through. It is the fact that everybody has a god that makes the first commandment so necessary. This makes human beings unique among all the creatures of the earth. No animal has ever revealed a god-shaped blank in their soul. No animal has ever been seen praying or doing anything that could be interpreted as praying. No animals have ever got together and tried to start a religion of any kind. Animals show no awareness whatever of the need to relate their lives to some centre of love and worship.

It is the need of every human being for a god that makes it terribly important to find the *right* one. But somebody could say to me, "A lot of people today are getting on very well without any god. There is less religion around, fewer people go to church, fewer people talk about God, most of my neighbours seem to get on fine without a God." But don't make any mistake about this. They are *not* getting on without a god. They may not come to church, they may not read their Bible, they may never mention the word "God", but every one of them is desperately trying to fill the god-shaped blank in their soul.

The important question to ask people is this: what is the name of your God? If you are having problems talking to an atheist, or anyone else, get them to write down the name of their god. If they have difficulty thinking of the name, say, "What is the last thing that you would like to lose or the last person? What is your most precious affection? Write that down and you've got the name of your god." It is not whether you believe in *a* god that matters. It's the *name* of the god you believe in that is all important.

There is, then, this double relationship with you and your God, whatever or whoever that God is. On the one hand, you look to your god to receive help, guidance, protection, meaning, fulfilment and satisfaction. On the other hand, you look to your God so that you may give homage, that you may have a focal point for your ambitions, for your affections, for your aspirations. All these need some kind of target and we are now going to look at the kinds of gods that people do have.

You can divide them all into just two groups: the supernatural gods and the natural gods; the things that are believed in outside nature and the things within our material world. Everybody has a god in one or other group. We either believe in a supernatural god of some kind or a natural god of some kind, but they are very similar when we look at them.

First of all, I am going to look at supernatural gods. It is very difficult today for many in my generation to imagine people believing in more than one god. For centuries, most were taught from childhood that there is only one God. We imbided this with our mother's milk – the assumption that there is only one God – and therefore when you talked to people about 'God' you assumed that they were talking about the same one you were referring to.

This has been part of our heritage. Most of us were brought up in a country where monotheism – belief in *one* God – was the normal attitude. Atheism, of course, means a belief that there is *no* god.

Most of us have not lived in a country where polytheism is the norm – and polytheism means belief in many *gods*. Fancy going down the High Street and meeting Mrs Brown from next door and saying, "How's your god today?" or even, "Who's your God today?" Can you imagine having one god that looked after Sundays and another god that looked after Mondays and another Tuesdays? – one god who looked after your kitchen and things that happened there, and another god that looked after your children and what happened to them, another god who looked after your garden and the plants in it, another god who looked after your business. This is not an unusual situation in our world. Many cultures have so many gods you are just in utter confusion. We are beginning again to realise what polytheism is like for a number of reasons. Historically, immigration has changed the range of religions in the land. So there are probably people living nearby who don't believe in your God, they believe in another. Some believe in a god called Allah, and that is a name you have never used in your church and never will. It is a name of another god. Some people are Hindus, and if you ask a Hindu for the name of his god he will give you a list of names for he believes in many.

These people who believe in other gods are part of our community. In my lifetime it has changed the face of religious education in schools. What god are you going to teach the children about when you have children in the same class whose parents believe in Allah, or Yahweh, the God and Father of our Lord Jesus, and a host of others?

We are returning to a polytheistic society in the UK. Migration is not the only thing that has brought about the change. The Western world is becoming increasingly interested in Eastern culture, philosophy, and art. So we are bringing more gods into this country. Some practise Zen Buddhism. Some learn Yoga. People learn these things and we are going back to being a polytheistic society in which people say, "My God is this", "Your God is that" – and use different names for their gods. This was the situation that the Jews had lived in. They were slaves in Egypt, and the Egyptians had many different gods. They had a god of the Nile, looking after the river that gave them life. They had a god of the hot sun that blazed down in Egypt. They had many gods, and many names for those gods.

In the ancient world, each nation had at least one god of their own and most nations had many. Everywhere you went, people were worshipping gods by different names. They didn't talk about "god", they talked about the name, and they always named their god. If you had asked anybody in many periods, "Do you believe in God?" they would have said, "Which one? Well; yes, I believe in this one but not that one." It is in that background – which we are beginning again to see and to understand when there is a wide choice – that God said, "Nobody else but me. No other gods besides me. It's got to be me alone."

We shall need to say this increasingly in our world, a world that's shrinking, in which people are becoming interested in many religions, in which interest in the occult is increasing, where many religions are having an impact – a world that has become tired of scientific materialism and is returning again to the supernatural, and to all the gods of the supernatural world.

Now can you see that this commandment is a blessing in disguise? It simplifies life. It gives you one object of worship instead of many.

I was once given a leaflet in southern Ireland, which told me which saint to pray to for any particular problem. There were 159 listed. Everything from toothaches to appendicitis to a broken marriage was covered, and there was the list of saints. What a complicated business it would be to have to look it up. "What name do I use this morning for this problem?" The sheer complication of praying to many people!

The first commandment is a great simplification of life. It teaches that you have only got to deal with one God. Isn't that a wonderful step forward? It is a liberating commandment.

It is an offer of a simple life. We learn that he can cover every need – by way of protection, guidance, fulfilment, satisfaction. There is only one God you need. You don't need any others. It is an offer. It is saying: you don't need to worry about all the different gods, just think about me.

We began this chapter with Acts 17 for this reason: when Paul visited Athens he said, "I saw that you were religious."

Everywhere he went, there down the main street there were temples, altars, places of worship, names of gods on every altar, all the Greek gods laid out in a row, and at the end was an altar inscribed, "To the unknown God". Do you know why they put that up? Just to make sure that they hadn't left any out.

One day an earthquake hit Athens, disaster came, and the population said, "One of the gods must be angry, but how do we find out which one?"

The priest said, "Release a flock of sheep down the main street. The altar they all lay down by is the god who's offended and you must then sacrifice the sheep on that altar."

So down the road went the sheep. Do you know they didn't lie down at any altar? Quite wisely, they went right past the lot of them and settled down in a field at the far end. So the priests all got together and they said, "What shall we do?"

Then a priest said, "I think there must be a god who lives in that field. We don't know his name though." So they put an altar up and I'm telling you the sober truth, that's how the altar got there. They put it up in the field at the end of Athens, "To an unknown God". "We thought we got all of them happy and there must be another one."

Paul came into that town and he said, "I've come to tell you about one God, the only one you don't know, the one whose name you don't know – that one at the end, I'm going to talk about him. He's the only one there is. He has made everything. He is not just living in one field. He made all that is. You live and move and have your being in him. I have come to tell you about the one God."

Do you know that is a liberating message? *No other gods* spells freedom. You can now get away from all the insecurity and fears of how many gods there are looking down on us, how many we have got to keep happy, how many beings there are up in heaven, we can look up and say, "The Lord our God is one," and that spells security. It did for the Jews and it does for the Christians who believe in the Jewish God. Our God is one. It is an offer of one God to look after everything.

At the same time it is a demand for *an exclusive relationship*. It is saying, "I will not be part of your life unless I am the only God in your life. I will not have any rivals in your heart. I will not have you trotting down the road to another temple to make sure. I will have your exclusive loyalty. That's the demand that matches my offer. I will look after every need you've got but I must be number one and alone in your worship."

Now that was the first commandment in a polytheistic situation. Did the Jews keep that commandment? The sad answer, if you read the Old Testament, is no. As soon as they mixed with people who believed in other gods, something happened – they fell in love with those people. The young men of Israel fell in love with young girls who believed in another god. It has been one of the most serious problems amongst the people of God all down the ages. What happens when you fall in love with someone who doesn't believe in your God? It was that more than anything else in the history of Israel that led them to bring other names into their religion. If you read the story of Elijah, you will read how he fought singlehandedly to stop them worshipping a god called "Baal", and how other prophets fought singlehandedly to stop them worshipping many other gods from those nations around them.

You might be thinking that some of these things don't really affect your life directly. I don't imagine that most readers of this book are going to rush off down to the temple of Baal. Most of us have been brought up in a country, where even though there were different denominations, they all spoke of the same person, though there were some variation of ideas about this person. The different denominations, if you went from church to church, were all claiming to speak of the same God, and they used the same name for that God.

However, there are now many non-Christian religions (and their places of worship) in evidence around us. Yet perhaps you feel that you are not likely to run after other gods (though some people do). You may have inherited the English tradition of believing in one God and you find it very difficult to think of more than one. Does that mean God's first commandment has nothing to say to you? I wish it didn't, but I am afraid it does. Let us look at what many people today use to fill this blank – this "god-shaped hole" – in their soul. They devote themselves to natural "gods" that you can see and touch, handle, hear – things that God has made. I'm going to tell you about some of them.

Come with me and visit a young man called Ken. He came to see me a few years ago and said to me, "Football is my god." His god was about ten inches in diameter, round, and made of leather! He admitted it quite freely. It was this little lump of leather that was the centre of his affection, attention and ambition, which he trusted to give his life fulfilment, meaning and purpose. Every spare minute he could get, he was worshipping this lump of leather. He paid homage to it. He gave priority to it. It took priority over his relationships, over his work, over everything it could. God had to separate Ken from his football just to get him free.

Come with me and talk to a dear older lady called Miss Clark. Miss Clark got up in a church in Buckinghamshire one night to give a testimony and she said to the congregation, "Babies were my god." What an extraordinary statement! She said, "I was a nanny," and she said, "I worshipped little babies. They were my life. I couldn't bear to be separated from them. I couldn't contemplate existence without babies," and babies had become her god! They were separating her from God. God had to separate Miss Clark altogether from babies to set her free from that god. Am I being practical enough for you? Both these two people were filling the god-shaped blank in the soul with something else that became their god. You can fill that blank, or try to, but somehow it never fits. Whatever you put in there other than God doesn't fit, but we try desperately hard.

You can put your sport in there, you can put your garden in there, you can put a motorbike in there, and bow down before it and give all your worship to it, and talk about it, and live for it, and polish it, and take it to bits and put it together again. It can become your god and so can your car when you get a bit too old for motorbikes. Your house can be your god until it is just an ideal home or palace, but you will still not be satisfied. You will still go on papering and decorating. You can make your business your god, and I know men who have so worshipped the god of business that they could not live without it, and what they will do when they retire I just don't know. They have sacrificed everything on the altar of their business, including their families in some cases. It is very easy to fill this god-shaped blank.

You can even fill it with a church and you can so live for the church that somehow God doesn't get a look in. Now these are modern "gods" and we are looking at something very near home. If it is not a thing, then you can put a person there. The worship of the personality cult is one of the phenomena of our day of mass media. Why is it that pop stars can get more worship, more emotional response? People who wouldn't walk down the road and wait ten minutes for a service worshipping God to begin are willing to get up and sit for hours waiting for a "star" to appear at an airport – why? So "worship" is often given to pop stars and disc jockeys and politicians – anybody folk can put on a pedestal and look up to. God says, "No other gods before me". Some parents worship their children. Others notice it and they say: "You know, that mother worships her child." Have you heard that said? Or maybe you have a girlfriend or a boyfriend and they have replaced God in your affections and become number one, and you are sacrificing him for them. You can make your husband or your wife your god.

You are trying to fill the blank and you can't quite, and somehow you remain dissatisfied – but God doesn't get in. The first commandment is "No other gods before me." I must be the first and the only object of worship in your life. It is a very relevant commandment. It has a lot to say to our day and generation. What we are saying is this: God can never be real to you unless he is central to your life. I meet many people who say to me, "God isn't real. I can't get through to him. I can't feel that he's there." One of the reasons – not always, but one – can be that that person does not want God in the middle but on the edge of life. They want to tack him on to all the rest. They want to have him as an optional extra when they need him. But God's commandment tells us: If I'm not Lord of all, I won't be Lord at all. If I am not in the centre I'm not going to be at the circumference. If I am not the first in your life, I will not be the second or the third. You will have no other gods beside me. That may be why people find difficulty getting through to God. They don't want a number one in their life. There is another number one already sitting on the throne. Number two, yes, or maybe even number three, but number one, no.

We have come to a big question now: why should I make God number one in my life? Can you give me one good reason why I should obey this commandment, "Thou shalt have no other gods before me"? Am I not free to choose my own god? Why should I ask God, this God who gave the Ten Commandments, to be first in my life? Why should I, a modern European, believe in a God of the Old Testament? I will give you the two reasons which God gave the Jews. They are still two basic reasons why you should have no other gods in your life: *reality* and *freedom*. Let me translate those into simple words. First, reality – he is the only God who really exists, and that is why you should have no others. So to have any others is to give your life to fantasy, to live in cloud cuckoo land. "Listen," he said, "I am Yahweh your God." Do you know what the word "Yahweh" means? It means *I am*. In other words, God began the Ten Commandments by saying, "I am, I am." That is God's name.

Moses, who received the Ten Commandments, said to God, "Who shall I say called? What is your name?"

God said, "I am has called you."

Do you know there was not another God in history called "I am"? Because he is the only one who is. All the others are not. That is why nobody ever thought of calling another God, "I am" – because he is the only one of whom that is true. You can search all religious phrases and examine all known religions of the world, and never find a God called, "I am" except the God of the Jews.

"I am" — every other god is a fantasy. All the gods of the ancient world were a fantasy. They were figments of the imagination. They don't really exist. I have lived in a Muslim country but I know that Allah does not exist. There are many sincere, devoted Muslims who bow down many times a day to a god who doesn't exist. It is tragic, but he is not "I am". He is not there. When you study all the supernatural gods who have ever been believed in, you are studying man's inventive genius, but you are studying fantasy not fact. They don't exist and that is why you must not have them before God. However much you feel sincere, however you feel that you are meditating profitably, there is no god listening. There is nobody but yourself hearing.

Now somebody will say, "All right, the supernatural gods aren't there but my motorbike is there. My children are there. My house is there. My garden is there. That's real enough." But is it? You can't say of your motorbike, car, business, house, anything – "I'm going to call it 'I am'" – because there is rapidly coming a day when you have to say, "It was." That lovely new car you got will be a rusty scrapheap in a few decades. If the person who lives in your house after you is not a gardener they will have a wonderful crop of dandelions in no time at all. That boyfriend or girlfriend is not going to be with you forever – even if you marry them you will say "till death us do part". That is not final reality. All other gods are just not real, not real enough to be God. In fact, all of the other "gods" – if they are real, tangibly, materially – it is likely that you will outlast them, and there will come a time when you are left without them.

I care not what you worship, what you devote your time to, what you feel makes life for you, one day you will be without them or it, and how can you call it a good god, a real god, when you are going to have to survive without it?

So that's the first reason: "I am Yahweh", "I am I am" – your God. I'm real. I exist. That's why you should have no other gods – because there are no others.

The second reason God gives them is this: "I am Yahweh. I am your God. I brought you out of slavery in Egypt."

He is not only the only God who exists, *he is the only God who saves and sets free*. Every other god will enslave you. There had been a time when those Jews had been chained and whipped every day, forced to make bricks without straw – heavy clay bricks that they could hardly lift – and their life was misery and their children were thrown in the Nile to the crocodiles. That had been their life but God set them free. God says: Now, no other gods. I've set you free. Don't go back into slavery. Don't become gripped again by something else or someone else. I want you to be free. That indeed is God's purpose in giving us this commandment—*that we should be free*.

Let me go back to my friend Ken. Ken plays football again now. He is a Baptist minister and he plays for a football team as his spare time occupation. But he will tell you this, "I can enjoy football now without being enslaved by it." Go back to Miss Clark. After some years without any contact with any baby, the Lord led her and put her in charge of a Salvation Army orphanage where she had more babies than she had ever had before to look after. But Miss Clark said that she could now enjoy them without making them her god. She was free, really free. What is your god? What is the name of your god? I'll tell you this, if it is not Yahweh then you are becoming enslaved to something or someone. Your life is being so bound up with that someone or something that you could never be free. You're not even free to enjoy that "god" because you are becoming enslaved. God did not make these commandments to spoil our fun and to make life narrow and miserable. He made these commandments that we might be free, and in his service is perfect freedom.

Are those two good enough reasons – that Yahweh, "I am" is the only real God, and is the God who sets you free? The ancient gods and the modern "gods" that people worship are not so different from each other. Study the gods and you find Bacchus the god of wine, and you find today people enslaved by wine. You find the goddess of love and people enslaved by sex. You find this god and that god and the other god and you will find all the ancient false gods are still worshipped today, if not necessarily under the same names. God says: I have come to set you free from all that and I've come to bring you out and I've come to give you life.

You may ask me what the name of my god is and I will tell you: Yahweh – the same God, but I've got a different name for him. The name of my God is "Father". How did I ever get that name to use of my God? The answer is because one day there was a Jew born who was his Son, and for the first time a man walked this earth who kept all the Ten Commandments perfectly and who would not have anything to do with any other god.

The result was that he was the most free man who ever lived. That free man enjoyed the things of God but was never enslaved by them. That free man who was God's Son called God "Father" and he taught: you can call him that too, if you love me. That is freedom. The law came by Moses but grace and truth came by Jesus Christ – and it is the truth that sets you free.

So what is the name of your god? Mine is "Father" – the Father of Jesus, and my Father too. What a God!

2

No Graven Images

Then as God finished speaking with Moses on Mount Sinai, he gave him the two tablets of stone on which the Ten Commandments were written with the finger of God. When Moses didn't come back down the mountain right away, the people went to Aaron. "Look," they said, "Make us a god to lead us, for this fellow Moses, who brought us here from Egypt, has disappeared. Something must have happened to him."

"Give me your golden earrings," Aaron replied. So they all did, men and women, boys and girls. Aaron melted the gold, then moulded and tooled it into the form of a calf.

The people exclaimed, "Oh Israel, this is the god that brought you out of Egypt."

When Aaron saw how happy the people were about it, he built an altar before the calf and announced, "Tomorrow there will be a feast to Yahweh." So they were up early the next morning and began offering burnt offerings and peace offerings to the calf idol. Afterwards, they sat down to feast and drink at a wild party followed by sexual immorality.

Then the Lord told Moses, "Quick, go on down, for your people that you brought from Egypt have defiled themselves and have quickly abandoned all my laws. They have moulded themselves a calf and worshipped it and sacrificed to it and said, 'This is your god, oh Israel, that brought you out of Egypt.'" Then the Lord said, "I have seen what a stubborn, rebellious lot these people are. Now let me alone and my anger shall blaze out against them and destroy them all. And I will make you, Moses, into a great nation instead of them."

But Moses begged God not to do it. "Lord," he pleaded,

"Why is your anger so hot against your own people, whom you brought from the land of Egypt with such great power and mighty miracles? Do you want the Egyptians to say, 'God tricked them into coming to the mountains so that he could slay them, destroying them from off the face of the earth?' Turn back from your fierce wrath; turn away from this terrible evil you are planning against your people. Remember your promise to your servants, to Abraham, Isaac, and Israel, for you swore by your own self, 'I will multiply your posterity as the stars of heaven and I will give them all of this land I have promised to your descendants, and they shall inherit it forever.'"

So the Lord changed his mind and spared them. Then Moses went down the mountain holding in his hands the Ten Commandments written on both sides of two stone tablets. God himself had written the commandments on the tablets. When Joshua heard the noise below them of all the people shouting, he exclaimed to Moses, "It sounds as if they are preparing for war."

But Moses replied, "No it's not a cry of victory or defeat, but singing." When they came near the camp, Moses saw the calf and the dancing, and in terrible anger he threw the tablets to the ground and they lay broken at the foot of the mountain. He took the calf and melted it in the fire and when the metal cooled, he ground it into powder and spread it upon the water and made the people drink it. Then he turned to Aaron, "What in the world did the people do to you," he demanded, "to make you bring such a terrible sin upon them?"

"Don't get so upset," Aaron replied. "You know these people and what a wicked bunch they are. They said to me, 'make us a god to lead us, for something has happened to this fellow Moses who led us out of Egypt.' Well I told them, 'Bring me your gold earrings.' So they brought them to me and I threw them into the fire and, well, this calf came out."

When Moses saw that the people had been committing adultery at Aaron's encouragement and much to the amusement of their enemies, he stood at the camp entrance and shouted, "All of you who are on the Lord's side, come over here and join me."

And all the Levites came and he told them, "Yahweh, the God of Israel says, 'Get your swords and go back and forth from one end of the camp to the other and kill even your brothers, friends, and neighbours.'" So they did, and about three thousand men died that day.

Then Moses told the Levites, "Today, you have ordained yourselves for the service of the Lord, for you obeyed him even though it meant killing your own sons and brothers. Now he will give you a great blessing." The next day, Moses said to the people, "You have sinned a great sin, but I will return to the Lord on the mountain. Perhaps I will be able to obtain his forgiveness for you."

So Moses returned to the Lord and said, "Oh, these people have sinned a great sin and have made themselves gods of gold, yet now if you will only forgive their sin. And if not, then blot me out of the book you have written."

The Lord replied to Moses, "Whoever has sinned against me will be blotted out of my book. And now go, lead the people to the place I told you about, and I assure you that my angel shall travel on ahead of you. However, when I come to visit these people, I will punish them for their sins." And the Lord sent a great plague upon the people because they had worshipped Aaron's calf.

Exodus 31:18 – 32:35

We come to the second commandment:

"You shall not make yourself a graven image or any likeness of anything that is in heaven above, or that is in the earth beneath, or that is in the water under the earth. You shall not bow down to them or serve them. For I, the Lord your God, am a jealous God, visiting the iniquity of the fathers upon the children to the third and fourth generation of those who hate me, but showing steadfast love to thousands of those who love me and keep my commandments."

Many people find great comfort in the second commandment. It is one of the few they don't have any difficulty with. I have sometimes told the story of two cowboys who went across the prairie one Sunday night to church. As they rode across the prairie, they sang and they whistled; they were very happy. They got to

37

the little tin hut where the preacher was giving his sermon, and he preached his way through the Ten Commandments. So when the two cowboys rode home they were very subdued. Until finally one of them said, "Well, I guess I never made any graven images." The other said, "I guess I never did either."

With that, they began to sing and whistle again. By the time they reached home they were as happy as when they had set out.

So maybe you feel that you are not going to get much out of this teaching. But just you wait! You can't read any of the Ten Commandments through the eyes of the Lord Jesus without feeling that they are a sharp edge of a knife that cuts deep, but it cuts clean and quick, and as a surgeon's knife in the hands of the Lord Jesus.

I have never considered taking a block of wood or stone or metal and shaping it and setting it up in the main room in our house or out in the garden and getting down on my knees before it and kissing it. I have not been tempted to do that. That is no virtue of mine. It never occurred to me to do that, so it is not something I have had to battle with.

In seventeenth century England, this commandment was taken very seriously indeed. These words about making a likeness of anything in earth or heaven or in the sea were taken so literally that many Christians felt that art was forbidden, that you shouldn't have such things as statues, or even paintings, on the walls of your home. Some of the Puritan homes were very plain and bare because of this commandment. I sincerely believe that they were mistaken in their interpretation of this commandment, but it has left its mark.

On the whole, Bible-believing Christians have tended to ignore the creative arts. That is a tragedy because it has left those very forms of expression to those who did not know how to use them for God's glory. But God is interested in beauty as well as truth and goodness, and being the Creator, and making us in his own image, he wants us to be creative people, creating in beauty and form, colour and music, things that bring delight to him as well as to us.

I do not believe that this commandment forbids two-dimensional or three-dimensional representation of things that God has made on earth. The reason I believe that this commandment does not refer to the cultural activity of art is that God himself, when he gave man the design for his tabernacle and later his Temple, included within the design embroidery, sculpture, and wood carving, and a number of other plastic arts. So there can be no doubt whatever that God is interested in art.

What, then, is the concern of this commandment? It is primarily concerned with our worship. The first commandment is concerned with *who* we worship: "Thou shalt have no other gods before me." The second is about *how* we worship: "You must not use graven images." The key phrase is, "...bow down and serve them". You must take this commandment in its totality. It is not just making an image, it is then using it as an object of worship.

Now there are three kinds of image that I am going to deal with. There are *material* images, which are the best known and the ones that spring to our mind most readily when we read this. There are *mental* images – just the same because Jesus taught us that you can break a commandment in your mind as much as with the body. And there are *moral* images.

But, first of all, why does anybody want an image? Why is there this desire to make a graven image and to centre our worship upon it? The answer is very simple: we tend to think in pictures rather than in words—that's the basic problem. So much so that when we are trying to understand something, when we understand it we say, "I see." Have you noticed that? It is because we think in pictures, and God has given us the great gift of imagination. We give thanks for that God-given gift. For example, a church building might first of all appear in a man's imagination and perhaps he builds a model of it before it becomes concrete and bricks and wood and metal. Imagination! We think in pictures.

Now here is the problem: when we have only heard words about a thing, we find it very difficult to understand until we see the picture also. Educationalists understand this, so visual aids are used in teaching. Visual aids are increasingly needed in this television and video age, in which we see more than hear. We learn more through the eye "gate" perhaps today than through the ear "gate", so we want to imagine a picture. The problem for us is the little word of three letters: "God" – it is a *word*. What is the picture in your mind as you read that word? You see the problem? How do you "imagine" God? As a very old man with a long beard sitting on a cloud? That is how many children imagine God. How do *you* imagine him? What is he like to you? What kind of picture arises in your imagination when someone says, "God"? Or when you read about him? Do you have any picture, or is it just a word that goes through your mind?

The trouble is that if it is just a word it is not as real as it would be if it became a picture, and you "saw" in your mind. But no-one has ever seen God. John's Gospel goes so far as to say this, quoting the words of Jesus, "No man has ever seen God's shape." The Authorized Version uses the word "form", but the Greek word is "shape". So what "shape" is God? I don't know, and that is the problem. How can I think of him? How can I imagine him? I need a picture; I need some kind of visual aid. I can't see God and I want to. Down the centuries, people have longed to see God.

Moses himself said, "God, just let me see your face once."

God said, "No, you can see a little bit of my glory trailing behind me, but no, you can't see me."

No man has ever seen God. We don't know what shape he is. We don't know what he is like. It is so difficult to worship a God you cannot imagine, a God you can't picture, and that is why people have made graven images.

We are not only thnking about images of pagan gods but also images of the God whom we worship. The first commandment was concerned with other gods, but the second is also concerned with those who believe in the only true God but cannot picture him and want to. Some people just give up and say, "It's hopeless. I can't imagine what he's like so I just can't understand." There are those who say, "Seeing is believing." It is nothing of the kind. If you see, you don't need to believe; *not* seeing is believing but it is a problem, isn't it? How to believe in one you have never seen and cannot even imagine. So people make images.

Now the fundamental principle of all graven images is this: that when you want to picture something, you always picture it in terms of something you have already seen and recognise. You always work from the known to the unknown. If you were describing sugar to someone who had never seen it, but who had seen salt, then you might start with a picture of what they did know and say, "Well sugar is like salt to look at." You start from something known. Therefore, if you were going to make a visual image of God, you might start with something you have already seen, which means that you start with something on earth, or in the sky, or in the sea—that is all you have seen.

Therefore, if you are going to make a visual image of God, you have to start with something that he made, and that is what every graven image has done. What you would not do is to make a shapeless blob of stone and say, "That's what God's like." So they started in the days of Moses with the golden calf. They recognised a calf – a young calf was the symbol of virility. It is the same kind of thinking that lies behind bullfighting in Spain. The young bull – the challenge, the virile animal, full of life, and sex, and power—the bull. So they would have thought: "The bull, source of life and power; God must be like that." They made a bull calf, and they set it up.

Now what is wrong with making graven images? Three things. Fistly, all of them reduce God. They turn the Creator into a creature because an image has to start with something you have seen and know; you have to make the Creator conform to the image of part of his creation. Therefore, you reduce the Creator, who is greater than everything he has made, to a likeness of one thing that he has made. You have reduced the greatness of God. When you make God into a golden calf, you don't sing, *How Great Thou Art*. You have brought God down to a manageable size.

Isaiah wrote, "'To whom then will you liken me? Or what will you compare with me?' says God." The answer is there is nothing in all creation that is like God. Nothing can be compared to him. When you look at the idols people have made, the images of God they have made, they are pathetic. You can't do that with God; it reduces him. God is "eternal". What kind of picture came to your mind when you read that? God is "immortal". What did you think about when you read that? God is "supernatural". What kind of picture does that bring to mind? Do you see the problem? When you make a graven image, you reduce him to that which is mortal and temporal and natural.

The second thing that is wrong with graven images is that you not only reduce God, you restrict him. From being the God who is everywhere, he is now a God who is here. As soon as you make a golden calf, you look over at it and you say, "That's where God is." It localises God; it puts him somewhere in time and space, and God is the infinite God. So it restricts him, not only in space but in activity. An idol is as dead. It doesn't move; it doesn't talk; it doesn't walk; it doesn't respond to you. It is a one-way relationship you have with an image. Isaiah says, "An idol – it can't walk and it can't talk. It can't respond. It's dead."

The third thing is that an image not only reduces and restricts — sooner or later it replaces God. God moves away to the wings, and *your* image is in the centre of the stage of your attention and affection.

Seven months after we were married, my wife and I were separated (in the goodness and kindness of the Royal Air Force) as I was posted overseas. So I took with me a framed photograph of her. It sat on my desk out there. It meant a lot to me as a reminder. But what would she have thought if, when she finally came to join me out there, I didn't bother about her, but went on gazing at the photograph?

"How about coming and sitting with me tonight?"

"No, I've got your photograph here to look at. I kiss it goodnight every night."

"Why not kiss me goodnight?"

"No, I've got your photograph here."

It sounds ludicrous, but that is what happens to every graven image of God. Sooner or later, God looks down and sees someone showering attention on that which was meant to represent him. That which men thought would be a help becomes a hindrance and a blockage, and diverts attention from God. I will never forget visiting Vatican City and seeing a bronze statue of Saint Peter with the bronze toes worn away by people kissing it. I just wonder what Simon Peter would have said if he could have just had one word with them.

A visual aid in worship tends to draw too much attention to itself. A representation of God will sooner or later replace God. Let me tell you what happened to a girl I knew who, after she became a Christian, hung a picture of Jesus in her bedroom. There is nothing in the Bible to forbid her to do that. She thought it would remind her of the presence of Jesus in that room. But a few weeks later, she took that picture and smashed it. She threw the bits into the dustbin. Do you know why? Because she found she was saying her prayers to it. Quite unintentional. She thought it would help and it didn't; it did the opposite.

Now that doesn't mean that you should never have a picture of Jesus around. Pictures of Jesus are used in Sunday schools to teach the children. But if you saw a child praying to a picture of Jesus, you would have to smash it. A graven image replaces God. It becomes a kind of substitute so that you look to the substitute. God will not have this. He is a jealous God.

He goes on in this commandment to say, "I have a possessive love for you. I am a jealous God and I am not going to share your affection. And to see you giving your affection to an object that I made – I just won't have it. The bad effects, of doing this will go down through your children and grandchildren to your great-grandchildren. It will have a profound influence for four generations. Damage will go down through your family through doing this." That is God speaking. He takes this very seriously.

Before we leave these material images, I want to consider religious symbols for a moment. Here we are in an area of uncertainty. By religious symbols, I don't mean representations of God, but reminders of God. They are in a rather different category. Jesus himself used religious, material symbols to remind us of spiritual truths. I am not a Quaker. I have great respect for many friends in the Society of Friends, but nevertheless they have carried this principle too far, and they neither have baptism nor the Lord's Supper. These are material symbols, reminders of deep spiritual truth—in the one case, water; in the other case, bread and wine. They are material, visible, objects, which are helpful in our worship, and which Jesus gave us. Notice this: that he took very ordinary things. Water – you can get it in the tap at home. Bread – you have some in the larder. Bread and wine were the staple diet of the workers. Jesus chose the most ordinary things lest we begin to treat them as special. If we are going to use a religious symbol to help us in our worship, it should be something very ordinary or else it will become too special.

Alas, even baptism and the Lord's Supper have been abused in this way, so that we talk of "holy water" sometimes, quite wrongly, or "holy bread", or "holy table", or "holy" this, that and the other. It is just water and bread and wine. Material symbols, yes, but that is all. They do not become "magic" in any way. They are not to be bowed down to—that is the origin of kneeling to receive bread and wine. They are not to be reserved as some special presence. They are simple, ordinary symbols. I think my general rule is that the more special symbols you have, the more you will tend to do with God what a graven image does with him. The more you tend to localise God, the more you will tend to treat God as so mysterious that he is not related to Monday and washing day and the office and the shop. That is why many of us prefer a building for worship without religious symbols except for those which Jesus gave us: bread, wine and water. They are just so ordinary and yet, so wonderful. So there is my rough rule of thumb and I am just giving it to you as my opinion. I do not believe that a church that puts a cross up is making a graven image, because they are not saying, "That cross is what God looks like." It is not an image to represent God, but as soon as people begin to bow to it or to give extra special attention to it (even by saying "touch wood") then it has ceased to be a symbol and become an image. It is a very fine dividing line and there is a constant danger of slipping over it.

Now let us move on to *mental* images. You can build an image of iron, wood or stone, and you can build an "image" of thoughts. The prophet Ezekiel realised that even though the Jews had got rid of all their graven images – the physical ones – they still carried the wrong images in their mind. He said, "These men have set up their idols in their hearts." In other words, they were still imagining a picture of God that is false.

What kind of a mental picture of God do you have? You could be in danger of making God after your own image. Do you excuse yourself when you sin? Then you make an image of that and say, "God will excuse me when I sin." Are you indulgent with yourself, tolerant with yourself when you go wrong? You create a mental image of a God who is indulgent with you and tolerant with you when you go wrong. It is an image and it does not correspond to reality. The Bible says, "Smash it."

I remember a lady coming to a service who said, "I've listened to your messages on tape many times. I built a picture in my mind of what you were like and you're not a bit like that." I did not dare ask her what she had built up in her mind. It would have just been too much. She made it quite clear that she preferred the mental image she had built up to the reality. But you have done that—you have heard about people and built up an image, then maybe you have gone to the station to meet them, and you just don't see anybody looking anything like the sort of person you were expecting. Your mental image did not correspond to the person as they were, so you probably missed them. In the same way you can build up a mental image of God that just does not correspond to reality – and when you meet God as he is, you are going to have an awful shock.

There is an idea around that God would never judge us for what we have done, an idea that God would never send anyone to hell, an idea of God as a sentimental old grandfather, more like Santa Claus than Jesus Christ – that kind of image is all too common. You listen to the conversation at the average funeral, at the bunfight afterwards. This image of God that so many people have just pulls apart from the God of the Bible. When you imagine what God is like, you must constantly check the image that your imagination has built against what God has said about himself, or you are going to build your faith on fantasy rather than fact.

Mental images are one way in which we can break the second commandment, but there's a third kind of image that I want to consider. The third kind of image is a graven one, but it is not graven with the hands of man, but with the hands of God. Do you realise that God knew that we would have difficulty imagining him? Do you realise that he wanted you to have a picture in your mind when the word "God" is said? He took that into account. Do you know that when God made the world and made the trees and the mountains, he wanted to set within that world a graven image of himself so that people would know what he was like? Do you know what he said? He said, "Come, let us make man in our image, after our likeness." That was the first graven image of history, and it was an accurate one. The name of the first man who walked the earth was Adam. The first man who walked the earth was a graven image, not graven by man's hands, but graven by God's hands so that people could have looked at Adam and said, "Now I know what God is like. Now I have a picture in my mind." That was what Adam was when he was made.

Now think of this for a moment. In what way was Adam an image of God? We know that God hasn't got a body – God is Spirit – yet there is a sense in which the functions of my body correspond in a very deep way to the functions of the godhead. That is why the Bible has no hesitation in talking about the eyes of the Lord, or the ears of God being open to your cry, or the mouth of God has spoken it, or even the nostrils of God have smelt it.

That is why the Bible has no hesitation in talking about the arm of God and the hand of God, and the finger of God, and the legs of God, and the feet of God, and the kidneys of God, and the bowels of God. The Bible talks about all these things. Our faculties and organs correspond in some amazing way to real functions in God. God can see, God can hear, God can smell, but it is a much deeper thing than that because that image is still here.

There is part of the image that has been lost. There was an image of God in Adam because Adam was made to live for ever and he was made to love. He was made for relationships, he was made for communicating with God, and he was made in the image of God. When you looked at Adam as he was made and saw what kind of a person he was, you could say, "That's what kind of a person God was and is." Wouldn't that be wonderful? But you know and I know that it is no longer true of Adam's race. Would you like someone to investigate your life in detail and then come to the conclusion that that is what God is like? The answer is, "No—a thousand times no."

What has gone wrong? That image which is still there in outline has been blurred and stained, spoiled and defaced. So that now you cannot look at a person and say, "That is what God is like." I know people who have told me that they just cannot bring themselves to use the word "Father" in their prayers, when they think of what their earthly parent was like. So we can no longer look at Adam's sons and say, "There's the graven image; there's the visible image of God. That's what God is like." So for centuries men were without a visible image of God. They could look at each other and they saw Satan. They saw evil and they saw nasty things. So they tried making golden calves, they tried to recover a visible image of God, and, of course, they failed every time because *they were making it*.

What did God do about it? He made a second Adam. He started a new humanity, a new human race. Here are some of the statements made in the New Testament about Jesus. Paul wrote in Colossians, "Jesus is the image of the invisible God." Writing to the Corinthians: "Jesus is the likeness of God." The letter to the Hebrews says: "Jesus reflects the glory of God and bears the very stamp of his image." In Colossians again, Paul writes, "In Jesus all the fullness of the godhead dwells in bodily form." At last, people again had a graven image of God, but God had graven it, knitting that image together in the womb of Mary so that, when Jesus walked this earth, people could look at Jesus and say, "That's what God is like. He's the image of his Father." Have you heard that said of earthly sons? You can say it of Jesus – he is the image of his Father.

If you want to know what it feels like to meet God, what his personality and reactions are like, what he feels about us, then just read the life of Jesus. May I recommend a little book to you – *Jesus, the Revolutionary*, by a Baptist minister from the southern states of America – just a little paperback but get it and read it. It presents the personality of Jesus in a wonderful way so that at the end of the book you feel, "Yes, I feel I know him as a person." In knowing Jesus, you know God.

One of the most moving things in the life of Jesus was on the night before he died, when Philip said, "Look, you've been talking about heaven, we're not even sure where it is or how to get there. And we're not even sure what it is going to feel like to meet God. If you would only just show us God, just show us the Father, just give us one glimpse of the Father, and we will be satisfied. That's all we want, just one look at God."

Jesus said, "I've been with you three years, Philip. Do you still not know who I am? You have been looking at God for three solid years. You still don't know what he is like. He who has seen me has seen the Father. Oh Philip, why do you ask, 'Show me the Father?' You have seen him."

But you and I are in the sad position that we cannot even see Jesus now. He is back in glory with his Father. We won't see him until he comes back again – then we will actually see his face. Jesus never had his portrait painted. He never got a sculptor to do a marble statue of him. What a pity, isn't it? If only somewhere there was a statue we could go and look at and say, "Ah, that's what God is like," but Jesus was wiser than we are. There is no recorded description of his appearance. I don't know whether he was five feet or six feet, or six feet six. I don't know whether he was fair or dark; I don't know whether he had blue eyes or brown eyes (probably dark and brown). Nobody does know except those who were there at the time.

What am I going to do now? I can't see God. I can't see

Jesus. I'm stuck! Or am I? God then began to create people who are being renewed, being transformed, so as to look more like Jesus. Colossians 3: "Put on the new nature, which is being renewed in knowledge after the image of its creator." Romans 8: "He predestined us to be conformed to the image of his son." 1 Corinthians 15: "Just as we have borne the image of the man of dust, so we shall bear the image of the man from heaven." 2 Corinthians 3: "We all with unveiled face, reflecting as in a mirror the glory of the Lord, are being transformed into the same image from one degree of glory to another." Do you get the message? God wants people to see something about himself not by taking a lump of stone or metal, not with imaginative ideas that are sheer speculation, but by people who are being changed. It has been my privilege, over many years now, of serving God's people and seeing one and another of whom I could say, when I look at them: "I can see something about what Jesus is like and, because I can see that, I know something about what God is like."

3

Don't Take the Lord's Name in Vain

The year King Uzziah died, I saw the Lord. He was sitting on a lofty throne and the temple was filled with his glory. Hovering about him were mighty, six-winged seraphs. With two of their wings they covered their faces, and with two they covered their feet, and with two they flew. In a great antiphonal chorus they sang, "Holy, holy, holy is the Lord of hosts. The whole earth is filled with his glory." Such singing it was. It shook the temple to its foundations and suddenly the entire sanctuary was filled with smoke.

Then I said, "My doom is sealed for I am a foul-mouthed sinner, a member of a sinful, foul-mouthed race and I have looked upon the king, the Lord of heaven's armies."

Then one of the seraphs flew over to the altar and, with a pair of tongs, picked out a burning coal. He touched my lips with it and said, "Now you are pronounced not guilty because this coal has touched your lips. Your sins are all forgiven." Then I heard the Lord asking, "Whom shall I send as a messenger to my people? Who will go?"

And I said, "Lord, I'll go. Send me."

Isaiah 6:1–8

The first commandment was primarily concerned with what we do with our hearts, the second with what we do with our hands, and the third concerns what we do with our mouths. "You shall not take the name of the Lord your God in vain. For the Lord will not hold him guiltless who takes his name in vain."

The religion of the Bible takes what we say very seriously

indeed. Words are very important. So much so that Jesus once said that we will be judged by every careless word we have uttered – not every *considered* word, but every word that has slipped out when we were tired, when we were under pressure, every ill-considered word, those words which, before we knew it, had escaped our lips. We will be judged for that.

Why does God take words so seriously? We say, "Oh it was just words." "Just words"? That is not a phrase that God would ever use because for him they matter. God used words for two purposes. Firstly, to reveal himself. It is the only way we can find out what God is like. We can't see him, we can't touch him, and we can't hear him with our ears. How do we find out what God is like? The answer is: through words. If God were not a God who speaks, we wouldn't know what he was like. But God has – over the centuries – given us altogether in his book 750,000 of his words. Because of those words we know what he is like.

The words that you utter reveal what you are really like. If you want to know what's in a man's mind, then look deep down into what comes out of his mouth.

The second purpose for which God uses words is to change people. It was by his word that he said at the beginning, "Let there be light" — and there was light. It was when he said, "Let the sky be divided from the ocean", and it was so—just a word. It was when he said, "Let life appear, and plants, and animals, fish, and birds," and there they were. But supremely, God changes *people* by the use of words. That's why preaching is still one of his main channels for changing people's lives. People say of a sermon, "Just words." So what is achieved? You would be amazed if you knew what happens just through words, but they have to be God's words.

In the same way, the words you use are helping to change other people. Not only are words an insight into ourselves, they are an influence over others. Your conversation this week has helped to change the people you have met. You have left them better or worse by the things you said to them, but you have influenced their minds. Gossip is one of the most powerful things and always will be.

What if speech is used wrongly? If I use God's name in vain, and we will ask what that means in a moment, I am not only giving an insight into the state of my own mind, I am not only influencing other people for harm, I am also insulting the God I am talking about. Since you cannot hold a conversation in the absence of God or talk behind his back, to take his name in vain is to insult him to his face. Those who take the name of the Lord in vain give us an insight into their own mind and the state it is in. They are an evil influence on others and they are an insult to the God in whose presence they speak. That should be enough to deal with the rightness of the commandment.

But what does it mean to take the name of the Lord in vain? Let's just say a little more about what a name means. A name is that which marks a person off from everybody else. It is a bit disturbing to meet somebody else with your name. I recall meeting someone not previously known to me who had been a Pawson and had changed his name (before he met me). A name is so closely associated with the person who bears it that what you do with the name will affect the person. If you forget someone's name it shows that at that instant you have forgotten the person, that you have not been thinking about them, and that can be embarrassing. The danger is that we separate the name from the person and when you do that, you take their name in vain. Did you have a sandwich for tea? If you did, did you think about the Earl of Sandwich? For that is the name that you used; he was the first one who thought of a marvellous way of going into battle and eating at the same time. He put some meat between two hunks of bread. You use his name often, and you never think of the man. You put on your Wellington boots though you probably don't think of the Duke of Wellington when you do so. They are silly illustrations, but you see what has happened in both cases. You are now using a person's name without even thinking about the person. The name and the person have been separated. That may be fair enough if the person is dead and gone, but God is not dead and gone.

He is around and he is alive. To use his name in an empty, hollow way with no meaning in it is an insult to our God. That is what the phrase "in vain" means. "Vain" means: "empty", "hollow", "blown up like a soap bubble". You are using the name of God without any feeling or thought. That is what it is to take the name of the Lord in vain.

Let us look at five ways in which you can take God's name and evacuate it of all meaning until it is hollow and meaningless. First, and probably not the most likely: you may have committed perjury. One of the basic problems in all human society is how to tell when someone is telling the truth, because we are all master liars. We learn at a very early age how to tell lies. How then can you tell when someone is telling the truth? One way is to make them swear an oath. This is common practice, and you may have been to your solicitor and signed an affidavit or made some kind of oath guaranteeing that what you've said is the truth. It is done in every law court. Why? It is really saying, "Are you prepared to call God to witness what you are saying?" But an oath only works if you believe in God, and if you believe that he will not hold you guiltless if you take his name in vain. An oath becomes utterly useless where God is not seriously believed in. That is why I wish they would drop this practice from the law courts because it is obvious that most of the people who take the Bible in their right hand, have no real belief that God would punish them if they did not speak the truth. It has become a hollow formality.

If ever I were asked to take the oath, I honestly think I would ask to take a solemn affirmation, which is allowed as an alternative, which might surprise some people – when someone who does believe in God refuses to take it. I wish more people would take a solemn affirmation – they might mean it more. But perjury is to call God to witness what you say and then to tell a lie. In popular language, some used to say, "Strike me dead if it ain't." That is the same thing, calling God to witness and to punish you if what you say is not true. A Christian might say: "As God is my witness...." Paul says it in a number of his epistles: "As God is my witness I am telling you the truth." It is a legitimate form, emphasising that what you say is the truth. To do that and then to tell a lie would be to invite serious punishment from God.

When Jesus talked about this kind of swearing – swearing in oath – he was teaching that what a Christian ought to aim at is the integrity of speech, in which he does not need to swear to convince people that he is telling the truth, in which his, "Yes" is "yes" and his "No" means "no", so that you do not need to swear by heaven or earth or by God or by anything else. If you say "Yes", people know you are telling the truth. Always be suspicious of someone who begins every sentence with "Honestly", because if they are having to bolster up what they are saying it means that normally when they don't say that they are a bit shaky.

Can you imagine a society in which everybody always told the truth? I think the solicitors would lose a bit of business and there would be an astonishing transformation in a lot of relationships. There would certainly be no need for an oath in court. People would be asked and they would answer – but that is not our world. We live in a world of lies because this is the devil's world and he is the father of lies and he teaches us to lie as soon as we are old enough to speak. If someone swears, they swear by God that they will tell the truth, and the *whole* truth, because you can lie by keeping something quiet, and *nothing but* the truth because you can lie by adding to the truth. That is perjury and it is taking the name of the Lord in vain.

The second way of taking God's name in vain is through profanity. Such corruptions as "gosh" and "Crikey" may be less common today than in the past, but the expressions "God!", "Oh my God!" or "Christ!" are used by many people casually, whether to express surprise or to emphasise a point. There is much profane language heard in all media. Now what is wrong with this? Some point out that the speaker is not seriously meaning anything. People say, "You know it's just habit, I don't mean anything serious." There used to be a time when people would say, "I do it at work, but I wouldn't do it in front of the wife and kids." They had some conscience about this, but now that has gone.

Is it just ignorance or a sign of illiteracy – that someone has not been sufficiently educated to use words properly, and therefore falls back on the same adjective every other sentence? Is it serious or is it not? I believe that this commandment says that it is, and for this reason: that the very thing that is wrong with this kind of swearing is precisely that it doesn't mean anything. It is that you have evacuated the words of their meaning so you are devaluing language about God. If you use the names of God and of Christ in this sloppy, hollow way, then sooner or later you will influence others not to take them seriously—that is the danger.

Alas, there have long been those who get a kind of sadistic pleasure out of defying the conventions of the sacred. We have come through an era in which viewers got a kind of thrill from hearing somebody use bad language on television. It soon goes dead.

Today you tend to find that those who really know God do not say "My God", using his name, unless they really mean to say something significant about him.

The third way of taking the name of the Lord in vain is what I want to call flippancy. A sense of humour can be useful if you can laugh at yourself. It is when a thing is out of proportion that it becomes funny. A great, big, fat man with a tiny bowler hat is out of proportion, or a very dignified man slipping on a banana skin. Because this is out of proportion, we laugh. It is a good thing to laugh because your sense of humour keeps your sense of proportion right. Slapstick humour helpfully shows up how ridiculous human pomposity can be. Billy Graham, being interviewed on television, was unexpectedly shown two clips from comedy shows. One depicted a hilarious scene in which a religious character was tripping over his robe whilst intending to be serious – the usual slapstick. Billy roared his head off. He enjoyed it thoroughly. He thought it was funny because it was saying that for human beings pomp so easily becomes pomposity. He was laughing at human pomposity and the ridiculous capers we get up to when we want to try to be dignified. Then they showed him another programme in which two well-known comedians arrived at the pearly gates of heaven and got in and looked around for everything they enjoyed and couldn't find any of it. It finished up with one of them saying, "Oh hell!"

Billy didn't smile all the way through. The interviewer said, "Why didn't you laugh at the second?"

He said, "Because in the first you were looking at human follies, the things we do that are silly. But in the second you were laughing at the things of God."

The line was very clearly drawn then. Now there might be those who feel that Billy was drawing the line differently from where they would draw it, and who feel the church should never be laughed at, for example. Well the divine side of the church shouldn't be laughed at, but I think the human side is sometimes desperately funny. We get things all out of proportion, but you can see that there is a line to be drawn.

One of the dangers is that your sense of humour can run away with you to the point where you are treating serious things flippantly, and that is dangerous. Let me give you some examples. Death is a very serious subject. The Bible never laughs at death, nor should you. Death is your greatest enemy on earth; it is the last enemy that you will have to face. To laugh at it is to help people to run away from it, and not face it and prepare for it properly. It is to do damage to their souls. To laugh at either heaven or hell is to make people treat them as jokes and, therefore, as not being real, and not serious. But heaven is terribly real, thank God, and hell is terribly real. So we should never laugh about the furniture of heaven or the temperature of hell. One is beautiful and the other is horrible and both are meant to be taken seriously. Flippancy can do this. It is interesting that those who make jokes about God usually try to avoid his name and they talk about the "old man" or "the man upstairs" or "him up there". Perhaps they feel the remnants of a Christian conscience. There is a line to be drawn here.

The fourth way of taking the Lord's name in vain is something for which Jesus had no patience and little mercy: hypocrisy. That is to take words on our lips and in our mouths that are not matched in our lives and in our minds. There are two forms of this. One is where your mouth is saying one thing and your mind is thinking another. The other is where your lips are saying one thing and your life is saying another, and we have all been guilty of this.

During a service of worship, do you find that your mind wanders? I recall that happening, my mind drifting to an urgent problem that I had been thinking about just before the service, and I had to drag it back straight away. Now that is a form of taking the name of the Lord in vain.

I remember a man who came for years to church with his wife before he became a Christian. Before he was a believer I noticed that during the hymns he would stand and hold his hymnbook, but he wouldn't sing a word, and he told me why. He said, "I'm not going to sing that until I believe it."

I thanked him for not singing. I said, "I wish more people would take hymns honestly like that." So can you imagine the thrill I got when he sang? Now he sings and means it, but even after he became a Christian, he told me there was one hymn that he couldn't sing and that was, *Take my life and let it be, Consecrated, Lord to Thee*. The reason he couldn't sing it was the verse, "Take my silver and my gold, not a mite would I withhold." Until he straightened his finance and got that right, he felt he couldn't sing that verse. He was not going to take the name of the Lord in vain.

The fifth way in which we can take the Lord's name in vain – and this is the worst blasphemy of all – is to claim the name of God for some belief or some behaviour that God would not acknowledge. The dreadful truth is that professing Christians have turned the gospel upside down, and they have done it in the name of God. There is a healthy practice in the Church of England to begin a sermon by standing and the preacher saying, "In the name of the Father, and of the Son, and the Holy Spirit." To do that at the beginning of a sermon, but then to go on and preach the latest philosophy or psychology or politics, is to break this commandment.

If I am going to start by saying, "In the name of the Father..." then I must make sure that what I am preaching is what he says. This applies to our behaviour. We might say, "In the name of God, this is what ought to be done." The Inquisition was done in the name of God. The Crusades were started in the name of Christ. There have been "holy" wars in the name of our Lord. The history of the church is strewn with shameful examples of this, but we can still do it. We can be so convinced we know what is the right thing that we claim the name of God for a certain form of behaviour and we may be miles away from the truth.

We have looked at five ways of blaspheming and there may be others. If I were to ask you whether you have broken the third commandment, would you admit that you have? I would have to. These commandments really cut deep. God takes words seriously because to him words are something that distinguishes man from beast. My dog does not have the power of speech, but I do, and I can communicate things that no animal can communicate. The gift of speech is one of the marks of the human race. That gift can either lift me above the animals or drag me below them because my dog doesn't blaspheme. This gift of speech can take a man high or it can drop him low.

James says about the tongue that it is like a prairie fire set on fire by hell itself. It is like a fountain from which both blessing and curses can come, sweet and bitter water for others to drink. James goes so far as to say that if you have never said the wrong thing, you are perfect. The tongue is the most difficult part of the body to control.

So this crime breaks the commandment of God. Is there a cure?

How do you stop a forest fire? I once read a story of a lady in a village in France and she was a gossip. She went everywhere saying nasty things. Finally one day she realised the sin of it and she went to her priest. She confessed and he said, "You must do penance."

She said, "I'll do anything."

He said, "Well, go and pluck two chickens, put the feathers in a bag and walk down the main street and throw the feathers out down the street."

She did this and came back and said, "Can I be absolved now?"

He said, "No, there's another part of the penance. Go and pick them all up again."

She went down the street and she saw a feather here and another one there and another one there, but most of them had gone. She came back and said, "I'll never pick them up."

He said, "No, and you'll never undo the damage your tongue has done in this village."

Is there a cure? Do you know what the Jewish cure was? It is a negative one and it didn't really work. It was not to use the name of God at all — ever. Over the centuries preceding the coming of Jesus, Jews became more and more afraid of using the name of God and they stopped using it. At first, they substituted the phrase "the name" for the name of God. They used to say, "Go and pray to the name", and they only whispered it in secret. Gradually it so went out of use that today neither I nor anyone in the world has any idea how God's name was pronounced. We think it was something like "Yahweh", which has been transliterated into English, but not even the Jews know how it was pronounced originally. We know it meant "I Am" but nobody knows how it was said and so we have lost the name of God in the Old Testament.

In your Bible, instead of the name there is just a word in four capital letters – "LORD" – but wherever you see that word in the Old Testament in capital letters, originally the name of God was there, but we don't know it so we cannot put it there, it has gone. They cured the problem of taking the name of the Lord in vain by just crossing off the words "in vain". "Thou shall not take the name of the Lord." That cured it, but the snag was that nobody talked about the Lord. So just as he dropped out of serious thought by people taking his name in vain, he also dropped out of serious thought by not taking it at all. Can you see that it had the same effect? It was a negative cure and it didn't work. Do you know that's why they didn't like Jesus? He used this name so freely. They didn't even dare pronounce it. They thought they would be struck dead if they pronounced it. Jesus was always using it, "*I am* the bread of life."

They said, "How can you claim to know Abraham? You're not even fifty years old." He said, "Before Abraham was, I am." They stoned him for it, or tried to. When they came to arrest him in the garden, when asked "Who are you looking for" they said, "Jesus of Nazareth."

He said, "I am...." They fell on the ground, they were scared stiff. He had used the divine name.

At his trial they said, "Are you the Christ, the son of the living God?" He said, "... I am."

The high priest rent his clothes and said, "You don't need any further witnesses. The man's condemned himself out of his own mouth. Did you hear him call himself by the divine name?" They put him to death just for using the divine name of himself and they said it was blasphemy. It wasn't; it was truth. But you can sense their answer to it—that's not the cure.

Let me tell you the cure. It is positive, not negative. It is not misusing the name of the Lord or dropping it altogether – it is to use it properly. It is to get the name and the person back together again. It is to get them so close that whenever the name is there, you think of the person. If you do this, you won't use it wrongly. In taking the name of the Lord in vain you have taken the name away from the person and you are using it in a hollow, meaningless manner. Put them together again—that is the answer.

There is a new name for the Lord now. It doesn't matter to me that we don't know the Hebrew name for God and can't use it in prayer because we don't even know how to say it. There is a new name, the name that is above every name. It is the name of Jesus. That's the name of the Lord.

I know that people still take it in vain. I know that they use it when they hit the wrong nail with a hammer. I know that they use it as a "mild" expletive and I know they say they don't mean anything. That is the trouble – they don't mean anything. This is the name above every other name. It's the name of the greatest person who walked the earth and who lives now. Once you know that person and are in a relationship with him, you don't use his name wrongly. One of the first things that happens to a person who is converted is that they stop swearing. Have you noticed that? When they get to know God, they don't say, "My God" any more, or, "Good Lord" – because now they know the good Lord. If they used that phrase, it would be with meaning and full of significance and purpose.

How does this happen? Step number one: *remission of sin.* You need a mouth wash and only God can give you that. Isaiah saw the Lord, high and lifted up. He suddenly realised all the things he had said. He prayed, "Lord, I'm undone. I'm finished. You know what I've been saying with these lips. I'm a man of foul speech and I live among people who do it. I've picked it up from them."

Then came a coal from the altar and burned it away. God said, "There's no more guilt."

That is the first step. Jesus has died to remove the guilt of the things you and I have said, and to pay the price for them. So all my perjuries, and all my profanities, and all my flippancies, and all my hypocrisies, and all my blasphemies are forgiven, remitted in Jesus; that is step number one.

Step number two: I need more than a mouth wash because the mouth is only an expression of the mind; I need a mind change, a "brain wash" if you like, but not the kind that men give—something much deeper. A "brainwash" doesn't make someone good; I need *regeneration.* So is that the answer? Not quite, because the new mind still has to live in an old brain, and the old brain has such habits that, when I become tired or under pressure, old habits of speech can come out. They do not come from my new mind, but from my old brain. So I need something more.

Thirdly: reconciliation, a new *relationship.* Now I call God "Father". Would you talk about your own father in a flippant or blasphemous way? It is wrong if you do. The reconciliation has made a relationship, so now I am aware that wherever I am, wherever I talk, he is there listening. I am talking in front of his face, not behind his back so I just don't talk inappropriately about him.

The fourth thing is *revelation.* Paul in Galatians writes, "God chose to reveal his son through me." From now on, the name of the Lord is going to be on my lips in the right way. I will tell you this: you can't be talking about the Lord in the wrong way and the right way at the same time. You just can't do it. If you are using the name of the Lord properly then you won't use it improperly. That's the positive answer – to replace taking it in a hollow way by using it on your lips in a proper way. This is the cure. I would like to guarantee that if you learn to talk about the Lord by name properly, you will have no problem about the third commandment.

When you are baptised, you are given a new name – not your name, the name of Christ. You are being baptised into his name. You carry the name. When the early Christians were baptised they didn't just take the name of Christ on their life, they took it on their lips. Everything you do after that is to be done in the name of Jesus. Your *fellowship* will be in the name of Jesus because where two or three are gathered together in his name, he's there. Your *prayer* will be in the name of Jesus – "If you ask anything in my name, my Father will do it." Your *service* will be in the name of Jesus. "Whoever gives a cup of cold water in my name." Your *power* will be in the name of Jesus. You will be able to say, "In the name of Jesus," and there will be power in that name. Your *suffering* will be in the name of Jesus and you will need to learn to rejoice that you are worthy to suffer for his name, and your *glory* will be in the name of Jesus. It is all going to be *in his name* from now on, and the name of Jesus is now in your hands. Whether he has a good name or a bad name among people will depend on us. We have taken his name – not in vain, but with meaning.

When you take his name properly, you find that people around you begin to be self-conscious about taking his name in vain. Have you noticed that? It either makes them swear more or stop it, but they can't go on as they did. They've got to take sides because you are taking his name properly.

I have often spoken of a man whose fiancée broke off their engagement because she just could not face his bad language. He went home brokenhearted, got down on his knees and said, "Lord Jesus, can you do anything about this mouth of mine? Can you clean up my language? Then you do it."

He got back into bed, slept all night, woke up in the morning and felt no different at all. He thought, "What a lie, talking to yourself and calling it prayer – nobody there to listen." He went to work and he worked all that Monday. Then, in the evening as they went home, he and his friend, who worked at the next bench in the factory said, "Are you alright, Gordon?"

"Yes."

"Are you feeling well?"

"Yes."

"Are you sure?"

"Yes, what's the matter?"

"You haven't sworn all day."

That was many years ago. He and that girl now have a lovely family. He would tell you that he hasn't sworn again. You must not take the name of the Lord in vain. The Lord will not hold him guiltless who does. To take the name of the Lord in vain is enough to damn a person to hell if they had done nothing else wrong. But rise and be baptised, and wash away your sins, calling on his name.

4

Keep the Sabbath

When God began creating the heavens and the earth, the earth was at first a shapeless chaotic mass, with the Spirit of God brooding over the dark vapours.

Then God said, "Let there be light," and light appeared. God was pleased with it and divided the light from the darkness. So he let it shine for a while and then there was darkness again. He called the light "daytime" and the darkness "night time". Together they formed the first day. God said, "Let the vapours separate to form the sky above and the oceans below." So God made the sky dividing the vapour above from the water below. This all happened on the second day.

Then God said, "Let the water beneath the sky be gathered into oceans so that the dry land will emerge," and so it was. Then God named the dry land, "earth" and the water "seas", and God was pleased. He said, "Let the earth burst forth with every sort of grass and seed-bearing plant, and fruit trees with seed inside the fruit so that these seeds will produce the kinds of plants and fruits they came from."

So it was, and God was pleased. This all occurred on the third day. Then God said, "Let there be bright lights in the sky to give light to the earth and to identify the day and the night. They shall bring about the seasons on the earth and mark days and years." And so it was. For God made two huge lights: the sun and the moon, to shine down upon the earth; the larger one, the sun, to preside over the day, and the smaller one, the moon, to preside through the night. He also made the stars. God set them in the sky to light the earth and to preside over the day and the night, and to divide the light from the darkness, and God was pleased.

This all happened on the fourth day. Then God said, "Let the waters teem with fish and other life, and let the skies be filled with birds of every kind." God looked at them with pleasure and blessed them all, "Multiply and stock the oceans," he told them, and to the birds he said, "Let your numbers increase. Fill the earth." That ended the fifth day.

God said, "Let the earth bring forth every kind of animal: cattle, and reptiles, and wild life of every kind," and so it was. God made all sorts of wild animals, cattle, and reptiles, and God was pleased with what he had done. Then God said, "Let us make man, someone like ourselves, to be the master of all life upon the earth, in the skies, and in the seas."

So God made man like his Maker, like God did God make man, man and maid he made them. God blessed them and told them, "Multiply, fill the earth, and subdue it. You are masters of the fish, birds, and all the animals. Look, I have given you the seed-bearing plants throughout the earth, and all the fruit trees for your food. I've given all the grass and plants to all the animals and birds for their food."

Then God looked over all that he had made, and it was excellent in every way, and this ended the sixth day. Now at last the heavens and the earth were successfully completed, with all that they contained. So, on the seventh day, having finished his task, God ceased from this work he had been doing. God blessed the seventh day and declared it holy because it was the day when he ceased this work of creation.

Genesis 1

Now look at Nehemiah 13:15:

One day I was on a farm and saw some men treading wine presses on the Sabbath, hauling in sheaves and loading their donkeys with wine, grapes, figs, and all sorts of produce, which they took that day into Jerusalem, so I opposed them publicly. There were also some men from Tyre bringing in fish and all sorts of wares, and selling them on the Sabbath to the people of Jerusalem. Then I asked the leaders of Judah, "Why are you profaning the Sabbath? Wasn't it enough that your fathers did this sort of thing and brought the present evil days upon us, and upon our city? Now you are bringing more wrath upon the people of Israel by permitting the Sabbath to be desecrated in this way."

So from then on I commanded that the gates of the city be shut as darkness fell on Friday evenings, and not be opened until the Sabbath had ended. I sent some of my servants to guard the gates so that no merchandise could be brought in on the Sabbath day. The merchants and tradesmen camped outside Jerusalem once or twice, but I spoke sharply to them and said, "What are you doing out here camping around the wall? If you do this again I will arrest you." That was the last time they came on the Sabbath.

Then I commanded the Levites to purify themselves and to guard the gates in order to preserve the sanctity of the Sabbath.

"Remember this good deed oh my God and have compassion upon me in accordance with your great goodness."

See also Mark 2:23 – 3:6

Another time, on a Sabbath day, as Jesus and his disciples were walking through the fields, the disciples were breaking off heads of wheat and eating the grain. Some of the Jewish religious leaders said to Jesus, "They shouldn't be doing that. It's against our laws to work by harvesting grain on the Sabbath."

But Jesus replied, "Didn't you ever hear about the time King David's companions were hungry? He went into the house of God, Abiathar was high priest then, and they ate the special bread only priests were allowed to eat. That was against the law too, but the Sabbath was made to benefit man and not man to benefit the Sabbath. I, the Messiah, have authority even to decide what men can do on the Sabbath days."

While in Capernaum Jesus went over to the synagogue again and noticed there a man with a deformed hand. Since it was the Sabbath, Jesus' enemies watched him closely. Would he heal the man's hand? If he did, they planned to arrest him. Jesus asked the man to come and stand in front of the congregation, and turning to his enemies he asked, "Is it all right to do kind deeds on Sabbath days? Or is this a day for doing harm? Is it a day to save lives or destroy them?" But they wouldn't answer him. Looking around at them angrily, for he was deeply disturbed by their indifference to human need, he said to the man, "Reach out your hand." He did, and instantly his hand was healed. At once the Pharisees went away and met with the Herodians to discuss plans for killing Jesus.

Some decades ago I had the privilege of visiting the little island of Iona, off the west coast of Scotland. We went on the old steamship called the "King George V". It carries tourists and visitors to the Abbey. It was a Monday, and one passenger said to the captain about the old boat, "Well, this boat certainly wasn't built yesterday."

The captain replied, "Certainly not. We keep the Sabbath in these parts."

Away out in Israel I saw a kibbutz from the coach in which we were travelling. It was an Israeli farming community, and I noticed something strange about it. At quite a distance from the community buildings there was a series of poles, each about twelve feet high, in a complete circle around the kibbutz, and running along the top of the poles was a single strand of plain wire. It was not electric and it clearly was not a fence. I asked the guide, "What is that wire for?"

He said, "That is a strict orthodox kibbutz, and that wire marks the length of a Sabbath day's journey. They may walk as far as that wire and they may walk around once inside the wire, and that is a Sabbath's day journey. They are not allowed to go beyond it."

Outside an old Methodist church I saw an unusual notice in chalk, saying, "Open on Sunday". It had been put there by the demolition firm and was under a notice of sale of old timber and bricks, which you could go and buy from the building that was being taken down. I wish I had had a camera just to take a photograph of a wrecked old church with a notice "Open on Sunday", which tickled my sense of humour.

Sunday used to be quite an institution in England, for better or for worse. I don't think there are many people who would vote to abolish it altogether. Most people who get weekends off work are glad of a break. Over the years I have seen some big changes in Sunday observance, as deregulation has reduced the difference between Sundays and other days.

In connection with that debate a group of Bible-believing Christians, men of considerable knowledge of the Word, were gathered together in London to work out a Christian attitude to Sunday and to produce a book on the subject to guide modern Christians. The fact is that that group of men, who believed in the Bible as the Word of God, could not find an agreement on guidance for Christians today and finished with different opinions on the subject.

That is why I realise that the ice is getting thin for me when I speak on this topic. I have the feeling that most of us adopt an attitude towards Sunday that is either directly inherited from our upbringing or is in reaction to that upbringing, and that we owe far more than we dare to admit to human custom in this matter. To give you a little illustration, I was brought up to believe that it was a very good thing to do to walk through a garden on Sunday – that it was a nice place to be. But to pluck even one dandelion root while wandering around the garden would be to step over a definite line—that's the kind of tradition some inherit in a Christian upbringing.

Others have inherited a much stricter upbringing than I had in this matter and are in violent reaction to it. Man after man has said something like this to me – they may have been making it an excuse – but they've said, "The way we were brought up on Sunday when we were kids has put me off. You know you'll never get me near a church now. It was just one mad rush. Off to church, back, off again, back, off again, back, rushed meals and back to Sunday school and back to church. While Mum and Dad slept in the afternoon, we were off to Sunday school, and this all built up resentment." So there are many who are in reaction and it is very, very difficult for Christians today to come to this subject with an open mind, and to read the Bible with an open mind, and to see what it really does say, and then to work it out in daily life.

Now I'm going to be pretty bold. I'm going to be quite frank and say that you must take what I offer you here as my considered opinion and no more, except when I quote the Bible, and then you can take that as absolute truth and work that out for yourself. But I can be no more dogmatic than that on a subject that has caused sincere Christians to have profound differences.

First of all, I'm going to take you through the Bible in a kind of whirlwind tour, "from generation to revolution", and get the whole picture and see what it actually does say about this day of the week. Then, secondly, I am going to give you a lightning tour through two thousand years of history, looking at what has happened to Sunday over the centuries. Just a word or two about each era and then I am going to come to today and tell you how I believe we ought to approach this subject for ourselves.

We are not going to deal with public legislation. The Ten Commandments are addressed to the individual, not to society. The word "you" at the beginning of each commandment is in the singular – it is concerned with personal behaviour. That is why the commandment, "You shall not kill" refers to murder. It does not refer to capital punishment; it does not refer to war, but that is another subject. It is speaking to the individual: you must not take the decision yourself to take the life of another—that is murder.

"You shall remember the Sabbath day, to keep it holy." Let us look first in the Old Testament. The position is clear. For the Jews, the Sabbath was one of three things that made them different from everybody else. Eating bloodless meat was a second, and, for the men, being circumcised was the third. The Sabbath was one of those signs of their race that marked them out from the rest of mankind, and this sign was given to them by God, written by the finger of God, indelibly, in stone. That was good enough for the Jew. The rule was that one day out of every seven, the last day of each week, was to be taken away from gainful employment and given to God, for rest and for remembering him.

The reason given for this rule is that when God made man he made him in some sense *like* himself. We need to be related to God, and man does not live by bread alone, and if he works seven days a week then he is behaving like an animal, for the animals "work" seven days a week. This is something that distinguishes man from the whole of creation, because no part of nature that I know has a Sabbath rest. I found that to my cost when I went to work on a farm and had to get up at four o'clock every morning including Sundays to milk ninety cows. I wish they had had a Sabbath sometimes. The corn went on growing by itself but the cows didn't milk themselves so we had to get up and do it. Alone of all creation, men were given this rule and the people of God were given it.

KEEP THE SABBATH

So here we have something unique, that man is more than an animal and if he is going to put that into practice, then he has to get away from the business of work, and he has got to get to God sometimes or he will only live at an animal level. That is the reason given, and so seriously did God take it that he said anyone who breaks this law will pay the death penalty.

So it wasn't an optional extra. There were many subsidiary rules that God gave to illustrate what he meant. He told them that they should not gather sticks on the Sabbath, they should not light a fire on the Sabbath, they should not roast meat on the Sabbath, and there were many other things that he told them. But there were many other things that he didn't tell them, and so the Jewish scribes began to develop more and more rules about what could and could not be done. At this point the laws of God moved into the traditions of men, and that is a danger point. As soon as human traditions enter religion you are likely to lose the reality and the joy of what God intends as a blessing, and it becomes a burden. That was precisely what happened to the Jewish Sabbath.

I listed some of the things that the scribes said you couldn't do. You couldn't set a broken bone on the Sabbath. You couldn't administer an emetic on the Sabbath. You couldn't tie a knot on the Sabbath. You couldn't look in a mirror on the Sabbath in case you saw a grey hair and plucked it, which is harvesting. You couldn't kill a flea on the Sabbath, which must have made for lively meetings in the synagogue. You couldn't eat eggs laid by a hen on the Sabbath because the hen had broken the Sabbath law.

Now they didn't laugh, and the scribes who made these rules didn't laugh. They honestly thought – sincerely, utterly – that they were doing what God intended. Though we laugh at them, we do equally silly things. Out of utter sincerity to God we insist on certain customs in our religion that God never intended. So let's realise what can happen. The blessing became a burden, the day of delight became a day of duty, and the day which should have lifted men depressed them. The Sabbath was a day that you were just thankful to get through for another week; it was a burdensome thing. God had intended it for man's good, and by the time Jesus came it had become something that was for man's harm. Now that was the situation. A good thing given by God, it had been destroyed by man's playing about with it.

There is one part of the commandment which people don't argue about today: "Six days shalt thou labour." If you are going to be legalistic then you must apply that one too. If you are going to plead for Lord's Day observance as an *observance* than you ought to be agitating for a six-day week at the same time. Which tells us straightaway that we have got away from the legalistic approach – whether we like it or not, there isn't one of us thoroughly legal about it.

There are some professing Christians (the "Seventh Day Adventists") who insist on observing this law to the letter, which means of course that they begin the day of worship at 6 p.m. on Friday evening and finish at 6 p.m. on Saturday.

What did Jesus do? There is a very difficult ambiguity about the life of Jesus in relation to the Sabbath. On the one hand he was born a Jew. He was circumcised on the eighth day. He was under the law. Therefore he kept every bit of it. So his custom was to go into the synagogue on the Sabbath day. For him it was a day of worship. So he accepted the Jewish Sabbath: 6 p.m. Friday to 6 p.m. Saturday as a day of rest and worship. He lived under that law.

But he showed a remarkable freedom from the way other people observed the law. For example, he would never for one moment keep any of the traditions and rules that men had made for the Sabbath. He just ignored them. It was this that caused the greatest friction between himself and the religious authorities and led them to plot his death (as we saw in the Gospel of Mark). When his disciples broke traditions, he defended them. He said, "You make the law of God of no effect by the traditions, by the commandments of men." They had added so much luggage to the canoe that it had turned upside down.

Notice too that Jesus saw the Sabbath as a day of *restful activity*. He was far more positive. They taught: "It's a day to stop doing things", but his words mean that it is the very day to *do* things – to rest from your own work in order to do the works of God.

What did God do on the seventh day when he "rested"? He worked harder than he did during the other six days – because the seventh day (in Genesis 2:1) never finished – it is still on. The work of creation was finished in six days. I personally don't believe the six "days" were of twenty-four hours – I don't think the scripture demands that exclusive interpretation. I believe there were six "days" of God because the seventh "day" has lasted a long time. What is God doing now? It is not that he is still making things. He is working for men's good now. So Jesus, justifying a healing miracle on the Sabbath, said, "My Father works until now, and so now I work." He used that to describe what he did on the Sabbath. So the Sabbath day was not a day to get in an armchair and put your feet up, but a day to stop working for yourself and do something for God, and therefore probably for someone else. Jesus had this positive emphasis. They could have said "You are breaking the law because a man with a withered hand can come the next day; he can wait – it isn't an emergency." But Jesus spoke of doing good on the Sabbath, and that was what he did.

Had you ever thought that Sunday would be a wonderful opportunity for doing good? Going out and visiting someone in need, doing something for someone else? Would it not be a better use of Sunday to go and dig a poor person's garden than to stick your feet up at home and read a novel? I'm trying to get you to think the way Jesus thought, and get away from the taboos and the scruples that sometimes blind us to the real possibilities of the day. Jesus made it more positive.

Not only that but, strange as it may seem, Jesus never taught Sabbath observance though he mentioned all the other commandments in his teaching. In the Sermon on the Mount he went through quite a few of them. What he did teach was: You have made man the means and the Sabbath the end, whereas God made it the other way around – he made the Sabbath for man, not man for the Sabbath. You are making it something that is not helping but hindering. But I am in charge of the Sabbath even, and it is I who should decide what goes on, on the Sabbath. That is quite a claim, and only the Son of God could make it.

The next thing I notice is that Jesus rose from the dead on the first day of the week, a normal working day, and stopped Christians worshipping on Saturday for ever. Why did he not rise on the Sabbath?

On the day of Pentecost, when Jesus poured out the Spirit, it was a working day. That was what changed profoundly the attitude of believers. If the Sabbath had been to continue in its Jewish form, the obvious thing would have been to rise on the Sabbath, arranging his death for a few days before (for he decided when he died). It is as if Jesus himself was going to make a definite break.

We turn now to what believers did, as recorded in the rest of the New Testament. First, every Jewish believer in the early church did two things on Sunday: *worshipped* and he *worked* – because it was a *normal working day*. The weekly holiday was on the Sabbath. They couldn't keep a job and not work on Sunday. Therefore the services were in the early morning and late at night. If you think that when Eutychus fell asleep and fell out of the window because Paul was still preaching at midnight that he had been speaking since 6.30 p.m. then you should think again. It was because they had to have their services at four in the morning and ten at night that such things could happen.

So they worked on Sunday because they were Jews. But they also worshipped on Sunday and broke bread on Sunday. They celebrated Sunday as the beginning of something great. The Gentile believers, when they came into the faith, worked on Sunday too because there was no weekly rest in the Roman empire, only every tenth day. They got two or three days off every month, so the Gentile Christians didn't have a Sunday free either.

Here is the startling thing: Paul, the missionary to the Gentiles who was very careful about what he taught them, *never once told them to observe a weekly day of rest*. Have you noticed that? That may be an argument from silence, a negative argument, but the positive side is this: Paul actually taught them *not* to observe Sabbaths. In Romans 14 he writes: "One man esteems one day as better than another while another man esteems all days alike. Let everyone be fully convinced in his own mind. He who observes the day observes it in honour of the Lord, but why do you pass judgment on your brother, or why do you despise your brother?"

He writes to the Galatians, "You were in bondage before you came to God but now that you have come to know God, or rather to be known by God, how can you turn back again to the weak and beggarly elemental spirits whose slaves you want to be once more? You observe days and months and seasons and years. I'm afraid I have laboured over you in vain." The word he uses is "Sabbaths". In Colossians chapter 2 he writes, "Therefore let no one pass judgment on you in questions of food, and drink, or with regard to a festival, or a new moon, or a Sabbath. These are only a shadow of what is to come, but the substance belongs to Christ." Do you understand what Paul is saying on those passages? Observance of a Sabbath is a voluntary individual matter of conscience. There is no ordinance of the Lord, no commandment of the Lord. This was a shadow, and when you have the reality, the shadow does not matter all that much. The reality of the Sabbath is this: *the Sabbath rest of God*. The letter to the Hebrews was written to Jewish Christians. Chapter 4 says: the Sabbath is not a day, the Sabbath is the rest that comes into your soul when you stop trying to be good enough.

So this is the Sabbath rest that remains for the people of God, that he wants all of us to enjoy, all the time, every day of the week – to cease from our own works and to let him do something in us and that's what Sabbath was meant to foreshadow. When you have got the reality why bother about the shadow? When you have entered into the rest, why get all upset about "Sunday observance"? When you are resting from your own works and enjoying God's peace in your heart, why go back to the bondage of rules and regulations about days? Now that's pretty strong meat, and it tells me that Sunday is not the Sabbath. Let's get that absolutely clear. If you take the New Testament as the Word of God, *Sunday is not the Sabbath*. The Sabbath was a Jewish shadow, Sunday is the day in which we celebrate our rest in Jesus. It is a totally different thing.

What about the history of the last two thousand years? The first three hundred years of Christianity—no Sunday. Worshipping on the first day of the week, yes, but no Sunday, no weekly day of rest, and the church never grew so fast as during those three hundred years. Some believe that if we lose our English Sunday the kingdom of God would collapse, but don't you believe it. It never did in those three hundred years.

Then the emperor became Christian and one of the first laws he passed was Sunday is a day of rest. Well that was a great blessing to the Christians. Now they could meet at a godly hour. But then he passed another law: *you shall go to church*. It was in the year 305 in Spain that Sabbatarianism came sweeping in. It was not long before there were laws about the circus, laws about sport, and the whole thing came flooding in which we have assumed is the "Christian" thing to do. But it came through a Christian emperor who had the chance to make the laws.

It was through the Middle Ages and the Dark Ages that Sunday became a burden to people. It became a dull and an unhappy day. What may surprise you is that it was the Reformation which produced what we call the "continental Sunday". The Reformation leaders (like Martin Luther and John Calvin) introduced new thinking about Sunday as a day of freedom. In Geneva, Calvin, who is looked to as one of the great reformers from whom all the Presbyterians and the Reformed churches came, used to preach in the morning to his congregation and go and play bowls with them in the afternoon.

Don't blame the "continental Sunday" on Roman Catholics, it was Protestants who did it, and who gave freedom to the people of Europe in that way. It's a bit startling, but if you visit Switzerland and go to the Brethren Assembly in the morning, they will take you skiing with them in the afternoon.

It was in England that a new attitude came with a group of very earnest and lovely Christians called the Puritans, who wanted to make this day more and more, as they called it, a "Sabbath". It was under their influence that all toys were banned except Noah's Ark. All secular books were put in the cupboard, and *Pilgrim's Progress*, *Fox's Book of Martyrs* and the Bible were Sunday reading. It was through the Puritan influence that that kind of Sunday spread to the New World and ultimately became English law. Most of our Sunday laws go back to that period. It prepared the way for something that has caused misery ever since: the Victorian Sunday, in which you didn't laugh and children didn't make a noise, you dressed up in funereal clothes, and Sunday was a serious day.

It seems a great tragedy that from being a day to celebrate the resurrection and the joy it became a day which many people remember with some sadness, though there were those who did enjoy the family life that was fostered by that serious day. It was inevitable that the twentieth century saw a reaction against that. We have seen a sweeping decline in church attendance. We have been witnessing in our lifetime a desire to make Sunday into "fun-day", and then into "sin-day". If you read a typical Sunday newspaper read by millions you see what I mean. Why is it that the Sunday newspapers seem to be even lower in morals than weekday papers? There has been a reaction for which we may have been partly responsible. People have said, "We want to do what we like on Sunday." So they stay at home, they will watch television, they will do the garden, they wash the car – anything but come to God.

So what are we going to do on Sunday? There are three attitudes you can adopt and we find them all in Paul's letter to the Galatians: *legalism*, *license* or *liberty*. I plead with you to consider liberty. Legalism is to go back to the rules and regulations and say, "Don't do that, it's Sunday" – and bring up our children with a feeling that Sunday is a miserable day on which they must not do things. If they live with that they will react against it – and rightly. Legalism is not the way. It makes it into a miserable, burdensome day – an imposed duty in which sanctity very easily degenerates into sanctimoniousness.

The second way is the opposite extreme: license. I want to do what I like on Sunday. "If I want to do this I'll do it, if I want to do that I'll do that." That is what many people are doing with Sunday today, and it is not freedom. It leads to a boring Sunday quite frankly. One of the reasons there is a demand for more and more commercial entertainment is precisely because people are bored. Did you know that the habit of lying in bed on Sunday started in the Victorian era because it was the only respectable alternative to going to chapel? Let's not go for license either—Sunday is not a day for me to do what I like.

But *liberty* is to be free to let Jesus be the Lord of every day including Sunday. It is to do on Sunday what Jesus would like me to do, to let him decide what is done. That's the claim he made over the Jewish Sabbath, but he makes it over every day of your life: Sunday, Monday, Tuesday, right through to the next Sunday. But on Sunday I want to be free to observe Sunday. Therefore I must leave others free not to observe Sunday. I want to be free to worship God on Sunday, so I must leave others free not to. I want to be free to come to God's people and worship with them. I want to be free to have one day that's different from the others and especially for God, but I will not preach that as an imposition or an ordinance of the Lord because the Lord Jesus never told us to do it.

In line with Paul's teaching, work it out for yourself between you and the Lord, and do what the Lord wants you to do, not what *you* want to do. I believe that approach to Sunday makes it the greatest day of the week, the most exciting day, and the most delightful day. Like an oasis in a desert, you look forward to it and it lifts you up for the week, and you look back to it through the next week. It's a day of inspiration; it's a day of lift. I want to be free from my own works that I may do his works. I want to be free from making money to be free to make melody. I want to be free to worship God—now that's true freedom.

Christians who go to church today, thank God, do so because they are free to, not because there's a law in England, saying that they must go to church every Sunday morning. Christians are free to give the whole day to God not just two hours morning and evening. They are free to give it all to God. If they rightly and freely give Sunday to God, not as an obligation, not as anything the Lord has told them to do, but something they want to do because they love the Lord, every other day will be different too. Every day they will enjoy the Sabbath rest. This is what was enjoyed by a Christian of many centuries ago who wrote a lovely hymn with the line: *Seven whole days, not one in seven, I will praise thee.*

The danger of "Sunday observance" is that when you have done it you can go back to what you were. The danger is even within Sunday that if you regard going to a church service as having "done your duty" and that the rest of the day is your own, you have not entered into the Sabbath rest. You haven't enjoyed the freedom from self and the freedom from sin that is the true Sabbath rest of God.

I see Sunday as a day when you can enter into a Sabbath rest for the rest of the week. If you love someone you don't say, "How much time should I spend with my fiancée? Will an hour do?" Can you imagine anybody talking like that of someone they loved? If someone were to ask, "What's the minimum number of times you should go to church?" it would reveal straightaway they don't love God. I love Sunday even though for me it is not a Sabbath.

Christian freedom – praise God for it!

5

Honour Father and Mother

We begin this study with one of my favourite incidents recorded in the Bible. Fancy knowing nothing about the life of the Son of God for thirty years except one incident! Wouldn't you love to know how Jesus behaved at Nazareth and what kind of things happened to him in his teen years? We have seen Jesus when he is only eight days old, and then get another glimpse at the age of twelve....

When Jesus' parents had fulfilled all the requirements of the law of God [*That tells you something about Joseph and Mary doesn't it?*] they returned home to Nazareth in Galilee. There the child became a strong, robust lad, and was known for wisdom beyond his years, and God poured out his blessings on him.

When Jesus was twelve years old he accompanied his parents to Jerusalem for the annual Passover festival, which they attended each year. After the celebration was over they started home to Nazareth but Jesus stayed behind in Jerusalem. His parents didn't miss him the first day for they assumed he was with friends among the other travellers, but when he didn't show up that evening they started to look for him among their relatives and friends. When they couldn't find him, they went back to Jerusalem to search for him there. Three days later they finally discovered him. He was in the temple, sitting among the teachers of law, discussing deep questions with them, and amazing everyone with his understanding and answers. His parents didn't know what to think. "Son," his mother said to him, "why have you done this to us? Your father and I have been frantic searching for you everywhere." [*That little speech is so typical isn't it?*]

"But why did you need to search," he asked, "Didn't you realise that I would be here at the temple in my Father's house?" [*Do you notice a little thing there? "Your father and I have been frantic" and – "I've been with my Father." With a shock Mary realised that he knew who his Father was. She'd never told him the truth, and she'd always thought that he thought that Joseph was his father. Now she knows he knows.*] But they didn't understand what he meant. [*They were not the first lot of parents to fail to understand their son, even at twelve. Now comes the staggering thing.*] Then he returned to Nazareth with them and was obedient to them, and his mother stored away all these things in her heart. So Jesus grew both tall and wise, and was loved by God and man.

Luke 2:39ff [*my words in brackets*]

"Honour your father and mother that you may have a long good life in the land the Lord your God will give you."

I don't need to tell you that family life is changing radically. It is changing in size. The average number of children is now two to three. My wife's mother was one of thirteen. It has not only changed in size it has changed in scope. Most homes today have only two generations living in the home whereas not long ago many homes had three generations living together. Very often my generation were as much influenced by our grandparents as by our parents. So the whole pattern of family life is changing. Indeed, some are predicting that family will cease to be.

There have been many attempts to analyse the many causes for the breakdown of much family life. Behind them all, Satan must be rubbing his hands because one of his priority targets is to break down the unit we call the family. Why? Because when you break the family down you break down almost every other social grouping. This is the one basic unit – as a brick is to a wall. It's true in churches that the hard backbone, the core of many church fellowships, is made up of Christian families. We thank God for those who are Christians but whose families are not, but a Christian family is a unit that makes for a strong church, a strong nation and strong communities.

If the family breaks up, most other social groups suffer. If you read *The Decline and Fall of the Roman Empire* you will find an astonishing picture emerging: desperate measures of contraception, child abandoning, frequent divorce, change of partner. When the Roman family began to break up, the whole fabric of the empire structure was strained.

We are interpreting the commandments in the light of the New Testament. We have seen that a commandment, through Jesus, is radically transformed and fulfilled in a very different way for the Christian than it was for the Jew. That applied to the last commandment, the fourth, concerning the Sabbath. But when we come to this one we find that it goes right through the teaching of Jesus and is quoted verbatim six times in the New Testament, whereas the commandment on the Sabbath is not quoted once. So this commandment on honouring parents goes straight through from Jewish life into Christian life, and as it stands it is therefore a vital part of working out our Christian relationships in community.

What does this commandment mean? *How* are we to honour our father and mother? I address my words firstly to those who have fathers and mothers, then to those who have children – because I believe this commandment has two sides, one of which is written and one of which is between the lines. Undoubtedly, the first way of honouring your parents in the first stage of life is by *submission*—which is not a popular word. I have chosen it deliberately. I thought of saying "obedience", and then I thought "submission" would make you sit up more because it has a kind of ring to it that we don't like today. We don't like authority. We don't like anyone over us. We want to express ourselves. We want to be independent. We want to manage our own lives. But while a child is at home and dependent on parents, this commandment is a call to the child to be submissive to the parent. Call it obedience if you like. There is something profoundly unnatural about a self-willed child. It's not natural and it breaks up a home very quickly. So there ought to be this first understanding: "Children, obey your parents in the Lord."

Basically it is the same attitude all the way through life, but in practice, with the changing circumstances of age, the same attitude will be expressed in different relationships at each stage. There will come a time when that dependence rightly becomes independence, and then the honour will change – from submission to courtesy, and to respect. One of the great dangers today is that many young people may have had far better opportunities in life than their parents enjoyed. They probably have more knowledge and they are probably cleverer, but that does not mean that they are wiser. It is this confusion between being clever and being wise which can make a young person guilty of the worst kind of snobbery, which is to look down on parents. Years should bring some wisdom.

The kind of courtesy and respect that will follow in this second stage is just the memory that your parents have been around more corners than you have, and that what seems to you as narrow-mindedness is in fact an honest desire to let you have the best of life. It is in fact sometimes even a hangover from the mistakes your parents made. One of the things we parents do, and maybe I'm jumping ahead a bit now, is that we will try and push our children further up the ladder than we got, and therefore we try to force them to avoid the mistakes we made. As one teenage girl said to her mother, "What did you do at my age that makes you so worried about me?"– which must be one of the most devastating questions that has ever been asked, to which there is no answer. But you must remember that your parents have sinned and that is why they desire to help you not to. It is because they have been around some corners they shouldn't have been around, because they have regrets about it, and because their life was tarnished for ever afterwards that they have anxiety that you should learn the easy way from them rather than the hard way.

So it involves a courtesy and respect after independence is achieved – that you are still willing to listen and consider their advice, just believing that their experience of life might have made them a little wiser than yourself. Or just believing that their anxiety is to help you to avoid the regrets that they have. Every parent would say to you, if they are honest, "I would love to go back and be your age again, knowing what I know now I would give anything to go back." But in fact we can never do that.

The third stage is later on in life still, when the roles are actually reversed, and honour becomes supporting those who once supported you. Here there are difficulties and deep questions to work out, and you may have wrestled with this question, "Should mum or dad go into sheltered housing?" That's the kind of issue you have to face, but at least you have faced it in the light of seeking to honour them, whatever decision the Lord has led you to, and it would not be for me to tell you what you should have done. So we have run the whole gamut here, from submission in the early stage, through respect and courtesy in the middle stage, to support at the final stage. As I understand it, to honour your father and mother will change with the changing circumstances, but your basic respect will always be there.

Jesus Christ is the most perfect example I know of all three stages. Stage number one was during his boyhood – when he was subject to Mary and Joseph. They did not know he realised he was the Son of God, but, even though he was, he still became subject to a village carpenter and his wife. I don't know if Joseph and Mary sometimes made mistakes in bringing Jesus up. But I know he was subject to them the whole way.

Nonetheless, there came a point where he achieved his independence, and the Jewish boy achieved that at twelve years of age. I mention that because we used to have a fixed idea in our society that twenty-one was the right age. The age of majority became eighteen, but might have to be lowered further. There is nothing in the Bible about twenty-one and eighteen. The age in the Bible was twelve, and at that age a boy undertook full adult responsibility. He actually became a partner in his father's firm. He literally got about his father's business at the age of twelve.

I remember being in Jerusalem, at a morning service in a large synagogue there, seeing a little twelve-year-old boy, his parents sitting behind, bursting with pride. There was the little lad with his skullcap on and he was given the scroll and he read the law – he was now the son of the law. He was now honour bound to keep it. No longer was he a juvenile, he was a man. The pride in the boy as he read the law in front of everybody! The *bar mitzvah* ceremony was a big moment.

Jesus was taken to Jerusalem and achieved his independence and assumed that his parents would understand that he had achieved his independence because he never told them where he was going. That was perfectly right – he did nothing wrong for he was now an adult.

They should have treated him as an adult and said, "Where are you going," not, "We'll tell you where you go." So he went—not thoughtlessly. He was an adult now, and so they became frantic. Like a lot of other parents they had not learned to let their boy become an adult. They had not learned to let the child go, to stir up the nest and let the little eaglets fly for themselves. So, "We've been frantic. Where have you been? You've had us so worried!" That speech has been made from about 11 p.m. to 2 a.m. in home after home all over the world! Jesus just quietly reminded them that he was now independent.

The next verse is a remarkable one, "And then he came back to Nazareth and was subject to them." Even though he asserted his independence, he still gave them respect. It is a remarkable verse. The result – Jesus grew in wisdom. He was in favour with God and man. He had good relationships with his heavenly Father and with people. Those who want to rebel and those who want to say, "I'm going my own way just as soon as I can get away from here" are not usually the people who enjoy good relationships with God and man.

We move to the third stage when Jesus was dying on a cross. He is only thirty-three, but as he looks down from the cross he sees a mother who is going to lose a son. Joseph is now dead; Mary is a widow. One of the last things this dying Son of God did, in all his agony when he could have been totally preoccupied with his own pain, was to make provision for his mother and arrange for her to go and live with John. If ever anybody honoured father and mother it was Jesus. As in everything else, he was our perfect example. We are called to follow him and to let him live his life in us.

I believe this law is for parents as well as children. If it says to children, "Honour your parents...", it suggests some questions for parents: Are you honourable parents? Are you making it difficult for your children to honour you? Are you making it easy for them to despise you and look down on you? For the other side of the coin is that parents should be honourable. What does that mean at each of these three stages? It means, firstly, that they will make wise and responsible decisions so that the children do honour the rules that are laid down. These should be a minimum, but an understanding of "how we behave in this family" should be based on honourable decisions, not silly decisions, not arbitrary decisions, and not decisions that fail to understand the child. If the child is to honour in the form of obedience then I must be wise in what I demand by way of obedience. So at that stage the parent's "honourableness" will involve being responsible.

The second stage is perhaps even more difficult for Christian parents than for others – it is learning when to let your child go, when to let them be independent. You will keep their respect and courtesy by letting them go rather than trying to keep them as your child. There should come a time when you understand that they are now to be treated as adults.

Let me tell you a little story. I remember coming home one Sunday afternoon in my early teens – from afternoon Sunday school. I announced bluntly, forcefully, defensively, aggressively, to my parents, "I am not going to Sunday school anymore." Then I measured my distance to the door, and waited.

I remember mother turning around and saying, "All right," and then she went back to the book she was reading, which was just perfect psychology. It just pricked a balloon of rebellion just like that.

I thought, "Well that wasn't even a battle."

Then she said, "There's a good group on Sunday evening, the young people – you'd probably enjoy that. Go along to that," which I did. I thank God that we didn't have a battle, but that she just quietly said, "All right," and steered me in a right course.

It's this being willing to recognise when your child is saying, "I am feeling my way to making my own decisions. I want to be an adult." Sometimes they say it a bit early and the pressures are on them to do it too early. But it is a wise parent who knows when the time has come to say, "Right, you make the decisions now," and keep the respect and the courtesy. Much better that than to say, "Look, I'm going to keep you as long as I can, and as long as you're in this house I'm going to keep you this way." Then when they do get away, they get out of the family too. They don't come back for advice; they don't come back to talk it over. It's easy enough for me to give advice! It's like the man who had six theories of bringing up children, which he freely lectured upon until he got six children, and that was the end of the lecture.

One of the accounts in the Bible that seems to me the most amazing example of parental wisdom is this:

One day a young man came to his father and said, "Give me some money, I want to go away." The father divided unto them his substance. [Did you ever notice that? What a father! He didn't say, "Look, I know how you're going to spend that money and you'll never get a penny of money until I'm in my grave." That would have been a more typical reaction, but he divided to them his substance, and sadly watched his boy go off with the money knowing that he would be penniless very quickly – he knew that boy. But he would rather have him come back later – penniless, yes – but to a place where he knew there was help and love, rather than have him chained to the home.]

The third stage may come if you reach the point where you need the support of your children and depend on them. That really is difficult. You have to swallow a bit of pride. I remember my father once saying to me when I was a boy, "One day I'll sit in the car and you'll drive me."

I replied, "Oh no, Daddy, you'll be dead by then." (After all, he was at least forty and he had one foot in the grave and the other on a banana skin in my eyes!) To be able to receive help from those you have brought into the world may not be easy but it may be the right way to be honourable.

So there are the two sides: to honour and to be honourable. If these both sides do not coincide, there are real difficulties. Let me mention one problem: how does this apply when the child is a Christian and a parent is not? I notice that there are no "ifs" attached to this commandment. It doesn't say, "Honour your father and your mother if they are good parents" or, "if they're honourable." It is saying: honour them whatever they are like. There are no conditions or qualifications. Why? Is there a good reason? Can I answer that by asking which half of the commandments this one is in? A Jewish child learns the commandments on two hands: No other gods; no graven images; honour his name; keep the Sabbath; honour your father and mother; do not murder; do not commit adultery; do not steal; do not bear false witness; and do not covet. Do you notice which half this one comes in? People have said, "There's something wrong; you know it really belongs to your relationship to people not your relationship to God. It slipped over. It should be in the second half, but maybe God just thought of six for people and four for him."

In fact there is a very sound reason why it is in the first lot. Your honouring your parents is a vital ingredient of your relationship to

God. You should learn an attitude of dependence, love, trust and obedience in your relationship to your parents first. Those who have respected their parents will find it much easier to reverence God. They will understand their relationship much more easily.

I am saying always honour parents, whatever they are like, because you are doing yourself a favour if you do. You are learning the attitude which will give you most blessing under God. We honour in order that we may reverence God. This does not, of course, mean failing to do what you know to be right as a matter of conscience.

As far as the roles of father and mother are concerned, together they can give the child a picture of justice and mercy combined. That's going to teach the child something about God's personality.

At a youth club I visited, the leader told me before I spoke to the youngsters, "Whatever you do don't mention the word 'father' and don't mention the word 'love.' Not here."

Of course I fell straight into the trap. I managed to avoid "father" but I mentioned the word "love", and a girl in the front row made an obscene gesture to me. I realised that was a blunder.

Fancy not being able to use the word "father", so that they had no conception of God through what they had learned earlier. That was in most of their cases because the father was not honourable. Perhaps they didn't even know who he was.

Respecting parents can lead us to reverence God. The natural cause of life, in God's plan, is that having learned the relationship in a home we then apply that same understanding of love, trust, and respect to our heavenly Father through Jesus Christ.

Deserting God leads to the dishonouring of parents. Why is it that family life is breaking up? Why is it that many youngsters are getting into so much trouble? Why is there often an attitude of rebellion? Because we have left God out for so many generations now. We're now many generations away from God. You go back through family life and you will find somewhere, several generations back, a godly man or woman who had a profound influence on that family line, but now they have got away from God. No wonder parents who have inherited "secondhand" Christian standards find it impossible to pass them on to their children. They are trying to pass on the fruit without the root and it can't be done. You run out of Christian "capital". But, excitingly, some in a new generation are finding God again. There are people whose youngsters have brought them to church. A little girl climbed on her father's knee and said, "Daddy, when are you going to come to church?" Thank God that there are those who will be in a position to pass on faith, showing their children the kind of relationship that can be developed in which loving God is not a duty but a delight, in which Sunday is a good day, in which worship is exciting and full of love.

That is exciting, but the converse is also true. In Romans chapter 1 you find that when men give God up, he gives men up. When he does, disobedience to parents is what follows, among many other vile things listed there, which read like a police desk blotter. You don't have to search far for the explanation of why family life in Britain has broken up. They used to get married in church, then they said, "Why be married in church?" Then they said, "Why be married?" They used to say, "Why be religious?" Now they say, "Why be good?" That is not coincidence. If you lose God, you lose goodness. If you lose God, you lose these standards, and you can't pass them on. Even if you have inherited them second-hand from your grandparents, and live a fairly decent life, you wonder why your children don't. The answer is: you couldn't pass anything on to them. You've got secondhand standards and you haven't got God.

So, parents, don't think you can pass on goodness unless you know God. "Honour father and mother" is within the context of the people of God – fathers and mothers believing in God, who have been redeemed by God and brought by God out of slavery. In that context, God says to the children, "Honour your father and mother."

What is the reward? In the Old Testament, God said you will live a long, good life in your land. That promise does not go straight through to the New Testament. There is no guarantee that you will stay in your land and live a long life because you have honoured your parents. But Paul points out in Ephesians that this command was the first one with a promise attached to it, pointing out therefore that God has a special blessing for those who keep it. There is no doubt that every family in which this is done is blessed.

6

Do Not Murder

In the two passages of scripture which follow, you be the jury and consider the question: was this murder?

The first is from the Book of Judges. It is the account of a battle between the people of Israel and the forces of Sisera, who was allied to King Jabin of Hazor. Together they were attacking the Israelites. Barak, leader of the Israelites, had only 10,000 men at his disposal, and they were on the top of Mount Tabor looking down into the valley of Esdraelon where there were marshes. They could only fight on foot, and against them were mustered nine hundred iron chariots, which were the latest weapon of those days.

I remember standing on Mount Tabor once with a modern Israeli young man, and he described this battle for me and so identified with it, that as he talked I almost felt he had been in the battle. He said, "Now our troops were here, and there were the enemy down there. We rushed down in this direction and they fled over in that direction towards Carmel." The thing was so alive after all those years; he was identified with this battle. Here is what happened:

So Barak led his ten thousand men down the slopes of Mount Tabor into battle. Then the Lord threw the enemy into a panic, both the soldiers and the charioteers, and Sisera leaped from his chariot and escaped on foot. Barak and his men chased the enemy and the chariots as far as Harosheth-hagoyim until all of Sisera's army was destroyed. Not one man was left alive. Meanwhile, Sisera had escaped to the tent of Jael, the wife of Heber the Kenite, for there was a mutual assistance agreement between King Jabin of Hazor and the clan of Heber. Jael went out to meet Sisera and said to him, "Come into my tent, sir. You will be safe here in our protection. Don't be afraid." So he went into her tent and she covered him with a blanket.

"Please give me some water," he said, "for I am very thirsty." So she gave him some milk and covered him again. "Stand in the door of the tent," he told her, "and if anyone comes by looking for me tell them that no one is here." Then Jael took a sharp tent peg and a hammer and quietly creeping up to him as he slept, she drove the peg through his temples and into the ground and so he died, for he was fast asleep from weariness.

When Barak came by looking for Sisera, Jael went out to meet him and said, "Come and I will show you the man you are looking for." So he followed her into the tent and found Sisera lying there dead with the tent peg through his temples. So that day the Lord used Israel to subdue King Jabin of Canaan, and from that time on, Israel became stronger and stronger against King Jabin until he and all his people were destroyed.

Judges 4:14bff

Was that murder? Now let's look at Acts, and again we ask the question: was it murder?

All the believers were of one heart and mind, and no one felt that what he owned was his own; everyone was sharing. And the apostles preached powerful sermons about the resurrection of the Lord Jesus and there was warm fellowship among all the believers, and no poverty, for all who owned land or houses sold them and brought the money to the apostle to give to others in need. For instance, there was Joseph, the one the apostles called Barnabas. He was of the tribe of Levi, from the island of Cyprus, and he was one of those who sold a field he owned and brought the money to the apostles for distribution to those in need. But there was a man named Ananias, with his wife Sapphira, who sold some property and brought only part of the money, claiming it was the full price. His wife had agreed to this deception. But Peter said, "Ananias, Satan has filled your heart. When you claimed this was the full price, you were lying to the Holy Spirit. The property was yours to sell or not, as you wished; and after selling it, it was yours to decide how much to give. How could you do a thing like this? You weren't lying to us, but to God." As soon as Ananias heard these words, he fell to the floor dead. Everyone was terrified and the younger men covered him with a sheet and took him out and buried him.

About three hours later, his wife came in, not knowing what had happened. Peter asked her, "Did you people sell your land for such and such a price?"

"Yes," she replied, "we did."

And Peter said, "How could you and your husband even think of doing a thing like this—conspiring together to test the Spirit of God's ability to know what is going on? Just outside that door are the young men who buried your husband, and they will carry you out too."

Instantly she fell to the floor dead. And the young men came in, and seeing that she was dead, carried her out and buried her beside her husband. Terror gripped the entire church and all others who heard what had happened.

Acts 4:32ff

The sixth commandment is the first of the second group, concerned with the relationships between people, as the first group of commandments was concerned with the relationship between man and God. The first and most important thing for us to remember in our relationships with each other is this: respect for the sanctity of human life. All the other commandments in the second table of the law flow from this one.

When we begin to try and understand and apply it, we run into very deep difficulties. Dr Albert Schweitzer took this command-ment to a very wide field. One day, paddling up the river near Lambarene – his mission station in Africa – thinking about life, trying to discover its meaning, there flashed into his mind one phrase of three words: "reverence for life". On that phrase he later built all his philosophy and his behaviour.

He carried it to such extremes that he was reluctant to kill either vermin or insects surrounding the hospital at Lambarene, which caused considerable embarrassment and difficulties for the rest of the staff. He believed that "You shall not kill" applied to every form of life, and that only if we reverenced all of life can we really fulfil God's intention for us—a view that is strangely akin to Buddhist thinking. It is a view that is cropping up in the kind of thing that I once saw when visiting Sussex University and was confronted by a group of students with a petition to sign to save the life of one tree that was to be pulled down to make way for the new library. They were operating on this principle: it is a living thing—we must reverence life; we must not destroy it.

But I do not believe this commandment is concerned with the life of plants and animals. If we cut some flowers, we virtually kill them – a few days and they are gone. We have then certainly hastened their end. Call it horticultural euthanasia if you like! Nor do I believe that animals are concerned in this for many reasons. It's quite obvious from the Old Testament that God does not promote vegetarianism. It's also obvious from the New Testament that our Lord would sacrifice many hundreds of pigs to save one man's sanity, so I don't believe that plant or animal life is concerned here.

But what about this matter of reverence for human life – how widely does it apply? There are three areas of discussion. Murder takes place when one person decides to kill another. It is interesting that the commandment begins with a singular rather than a plural word. It is not addressed to societies or groups; it says "you", as an individual must not kill another individual, so the primary application is clearly in the realm of personal killing.

An area in which sincere Christians are not all agreed, though there is a majority view, is what I call "social killing" in which a group of people take on themselves the responsibility of taking life from a human being. One issue is capital punishment, in which the government takes that responsibility, whoever carries it out. Another is the widely debated matter of war, and whether this is ever a valid means of settling an issue.

Then there is medical killing. The two questions that have come to the fore are abortion and euthanasia. There is withdrawal of medical treatment so that a person dies through natural causes, but in recent years there has come in, in some countries deliberate killing, "voluntary euthanasia" which is not about the relief of pain but the deliberate, planned ending of lives by killing at a "clinic".

I predicted many years ago that euthanasia would be with us in this country in not many years' time. It is a living issue in Europe, and you may well find yourself chatting over with your doctor what to do about dear old Mum.

There are three possible approaches to this kind of discussion.

One, I am going to call the *sentimental* approach, which simply asks, "How do I feel about this?" Now that is the approach that many people, alas, take, and it leads you into some very odd conclusions. For example, I have been asked, "Can you imagine Jesus pressing a button and releasing a bomb?" My answer is: that is a question that is appealing to my feelings, whereas, if I am mentally honest and face the facts—that is exactly how the New Testament presents Jesus. You read the early chapters of the book of Revelation, and the whole of heaven is saying, "Who is worthy to open the scroll and release what is in that?" and we are told Jesus is the one who steps forward and releases on earth plagues and tragedies such as history has never seen. So while my feelings may say, "I can't imagine Jesus doing this", the Bible says he will. So you see how an appeal to feelings might be: how would you feel if you had to press the button on an electric chair? I should feel terrible, but that is not the answer to the question. So the sentimental approach that says, "My feelings should guide me, or my feelings about others should guide me" is, I think, the wrong approach.

The second way is what I am going to call the *social* approach. By that I mean to take on in the colour of your thinking the mood of the age in which you live. We have lived to see the sanctity of human life progressively deteriorate. We have seen life become cheap—it is no coincidence that following the abolition of capital punishment we have seen the introduction of widespread abortion and the increase in violence. Every one of those things, though they sound contradictory when I first mention them, is due to a lessening of the sanctity of human life. I know that the abolition of capital punishment was made in the name of preserving human life, but I honestly believe that it has had precisely the opposite effect, and that we are learning the hard way that a mistake has been made.

Regardless of that particular issue, the general value placed on human life is going down. One reason is that the mass media are constantly conveying a message that human life is cheap. You are seeing bodies lie around, you are seeing people blown up, and you go on eating your food while you watch. This is having a very subtle and dangerous effect on our thinking. You can now watch violence without the horror that once you felt. We live in an age when violent attack on human life is thought to be good entertainment, and people will pay to watch it.

Now in this atmosphere and the lowering of the sanctity of human life, anything goes. I predict that soon there will be those who will feel no worse about putting granny down as putting their favourite dog down. That is what we are heading for. It is only a matter of time until people are treating each other as animals. I expect if you have ever had a dog put down you felt it very deeply, and you were very sad and came home feeling it was the best thing to do for dear old Bonzo....

Society is moving away rapidly from God's way of thinking, and therefore to talk about capital punishment or to talk against euthanasia will certainly draw the charge very quickly that you are old-fashioned, on this terrible delusion that the latest view is the best, and that as you go on through society's history you become more enlightened, more modern, more broad-minded, and that if you cling to old ideas you really are out of date.

There is a third approach, the scriptural approach, which says *how does God feel?* I approach these issues from that point of view. I do not claim to know God's mind on some issues. The Bible does not mention abortion and euthanasia. So we have to feel our way into God's mind on such matters, but he does talk about war, capital punishment and murder.

So let us go to the most obvious question of murder—where one person deliberately, knowingly, maliciously and intentionally takes the life of another. God thinks differently about manslaughter and murder. The Bible is quite clear about that. That is why God in his mercy provided six cities of refuge in Israel where a man who had *accidentally* killed another without malice aforethought could flee for refuge and be given a fair trial.

So what we are considering now is *killing with malice aforethought.* Not necessarily long aforethought, for murders are in two categories—the "cold-blooded" and the "hot-blooded". The former is probably thought out long before, the latter is thought out quickly, but the two are both thought out beforehand and a person is attacked with the intention of taking their life from them. Both are murder, and manslaughter is a different thing.

There are two interesting things in the Bible about murder: why it is wrong and how it is to be punished. Why is it wrong? The humanistic view is that murder is wrong because it is theft.

It is the supreme robbery. It is to take from a person their most precious possession. It is one thing to rob someone of money or goods, but to take away a life is the supreme act of theft, and you can never give it back.

Now supposing someone had asked you (though it is probably not a question that would occur to you): *why* is it wrong to murder someone? The Bible never mentions theft of a life. It never suggests that the reason it is wrong is because you are taking a person's life away from them. It never mentions that it's wrong because you're robbing someone of their most precious possession. It never says that it's wrong because it cannot be undone. It says that *it is wrong because it is sacrilege*. What is sacrilege? It is to lift up your hand against something holy. It is serious to rob a person of life and of that which is their most precious possession and something you can never give back, but the serious thing about murder is that you are doing something *against God's image*. It is not that it is a human being you are doing this to, it is that it is the image of God you are doing it to, and this is why from the very early pages of the Bible it is stated that a man who sheds another man's blood is lifting his hand against God, for that man is in God's image. An animal is not in God's image. A flower is not in God's image, beautiful though it may be, but every person you see is made in the image of God. The image may be defaced, it may be deformed, it may be spoiled and stained, but it is still there and it could be restored by grace. In touching that, you are touching God's image. That is totally different from the humanist arguments.

The second unusual thing about the Bible's teaching is how murder should be punished. We go back beyond the Ten Commandments, way back to Abraham, beyond Abraham, way back to Noah, and we find this simple statement, "Whoever sheds man's blood, by man shall his blood be shed." There it is, and it is God speaking, not Noah. Having destroyed a whole society himself, God is in effect saying: Noah, after that, the only way for human beings to keep the sanctity of life intact is for the murderer to lose his life. That concerns murder with malice aforethought, and it goes right on through the Bible.

Those who feel that to kill a murderer is wrong because it is simply "adding one sin to another" and "two wrongs don't make a right" have never studied Exodus 20, which says, "You shall not kill." Exodus 21, where God is still speaking to Moses on the same occasion says, "If a man deliberately attacks another, intending to kill him, then drag him even from my altar and kill him." Nothing could be clearer.

Now this is the point, I believe, on which this whole discussion hangs. If you once grant that capital punishment was God's will, then you have granted that justice is even more important than human life. If you grant that, then you have got the answer to all the questions that I raised under the form of social killing. If human life is the highest value on the scale, and justice comes second to that, then of course you would not kill a murderer, but if justice is above even the value of a human life, then you would. I am telling you that justice is above human life, because God is just. This is the principle on which God has worked from the very beginning, and he will maintain that until the very end.

Do you see that nobody would ever die unless God had pronounced the death sentence on that person? Death is not a normal, biological, scientific event. Scientists will tell you there is no reason whatever within your frame why you should die. Yet at the moment you are dying. The cells of your body are dying and your body is – by food and fresh air and rest – replacing those dying cells with new cells and you can go on doing that comfortably. I am beginning to lose the battle. My teeth and hair tell me that! There is no biological or scientifically discovered reason whatever why we should lose this battle provided we go on feeding ourselves, getting plenty of fresh air and exercise. Why can we not go on replacing? There is within our biological make-up a clock that starts running down, and according to the Bible that clock is not there naturally – God put it there, and it was a death sentence for sin. Death is an unnatural event, and we know it is in our hearts. That very first death to the very last is God's sentence on sin, and it has been that way all the way through. For God, justice is even more important than human life, because he is just.

The Roman authorities had the symbol of the sword which was used for defending the empire and beheading criminals – that symbol is described in the New Testament as the symbol of a ministry of God for the restraining and punishing of evildoers. You can tell me that capital punishment doesn't reform the criminal—I agree. You can tell me that it doesn't deter other murderers—I agree. But neither of those is the point. The point is the sanctity of life – of the divine image in man that has been attacked, and it is justice that is more important than that.

If that is granted then all the other things follow. Christians have never believed that all war is right. Neither have the majority of Christians believed that all war was wrong. The more difficult course in between has always been the course that the people of God in the Old Testament had to follow. God made it clear that in some situations if justice was to be done then war would have to be done. On other occasions they rushed into war and God told them that was not a just attack, and that they would not win it and that they would suffer. They were not told by God that all war is right or that all war is wrong. They were told by God justice is always right and sometimes it may be necessary to use the ultimate sanction of physical force to maintain the principle of justice, and all through the Bible that is what God did.

That is why when Paul was in the dock in a court on a false charge which (had it not been false) would have deserved the death penalty, he said in the dock, "I refuse not to die if I am guilty...." That's St. Paul speaking. Quite a statement from the leading Christian theologian and thinker of the first century! Now one intriguing question follows—granted that it is necessary for the ultimate sanction to be used in human society, should Christians use it? Should they not leave it to unbelievers? I frankly think that is a cowardly way out, for which there is no warrant whatever in scripture. The Christian is a citizen of two kingdoms, earthly and heavenly, and the Bible teaches that you have responsibilities to both. You cannot opt out of your earthly responsibilities because you now belong to heaven. It is true that you must never use physical force in the service of the heavenly kingdom. Jesus said to Pilate, "My kingdom is not of this world, or else my servants would fight."

The problem is that we still belong to both, and we have to render to Caesar what is Caesar's and render to God what is God's. The easy course is to join the army and fight any war that we are told to fight. The more difficult thing is to be a conscientious objector and not join the army at all, or only the medical corps, or serve on the farm – or, as in the First World War, go to prison for your convictions. The most difficult course of all is to be willing to fight when justice warrants it, and to be willing not to when it doesn't.

I was called in as an RAF Chaplain to one situation that arose over Suez. I was out in the Middle East during the Suez Crisis. As a Chaplain I had it easy, because I was a non-combatant. I would never be called upon to fight, and indeed it was illegal for me to fire a weapon, so I suppose if the enemy did get us, I would be the first prisoner. So I was out of it. Chaplains in the forces are not committed to the policy of the forces. They are only there to help the men who otherwise might not get the gospel. But the men were in it, and at the time of Suez a man refused to take off in a Canberra bomber to go and bomb Suez, because he said, "This is not a just situation." That had repercussions right through our troops, and I was counselling men on this issue. Many wars present such issues.

We move to the medical world, and from what I would call "justice killing", which would seem to me to have considerable biblical warrant, to so-called "mercy killing". We have to face the whole issue squarely, and I can only tell you that on my understanding of the Bible I cannot see that we have the right to shorten a person's existence. I know that we have discovered medical means of keeping them alive longer, but I am scared stiff of the long-term effect of widespread euthanasia. First, think of the effect on the people themselves — have not most of us reached points where we wanted to go, if we are honest? There have been times when life just got too much for us, and yet somehow we got through and we are just thankful that neither we nor anybody else made us take that decision, and we realise that God had more for us to do. We have all been down, some more than others.

I also tremble for the effect on relatives. The kind of situation usually mentioned is where a wealthy relative is elderly and wants to go, and that money will not come to the family until they do. There is a pressure there that I tremble about. But I tremble most at the general effect on overall society, and that while we consider only the individual's case, a strong emotional case can be made out for helping them. Nevertheless, the long-term effect on the general society will be so to lower the value of human life that other more terrible things will follow on behind. I give you this as my opinion. I have no word from the Bible for it.

In conclusion, I want to tell you that this commandment

concerns something that I believe applies to almost every one of us. I am going to tell you what Jesus said this commandment meant. He taught that there is more than one way of murdering someone: you can murder them in *feeling*; you can murder them in *thought*, and you can murder them in *word*, and they are just as serious as murdering in deed.

The three cases he mentioned were *anger*, *arrogance* and *abuse*. Jesus said, "If you've ever been angry with someone without a just cause, you are a murderer." You are, and you are in danger of hell fire if you have ever been angry with someone without a cause – a good reason. How many of us does that make into murderers? *Anger* is murder in emotion. You have wished somebody dead, and if your anger didn't display itself in deed, the fact that it was there means that within your heart is all the potential of a murderer.

The second way is to murder someone in thought by *arrogance*. Do you know that Jesus taught that snobbery is murder? To despise someone is to destroy them. To look down on them because you have more financial or more social or more intellectual qualities about you—to do that is murder; to treat them as beneath you. Why is it murder? Because you have forgotten that they are made in the image of God. That man in the gutter in his rags is made in the image of God, and if you despise him you murder him—that's what Jesus taught.

The final way he said is *abuse*. Have you ever called someone a moron? Have you ever called someone a fool and meant by that, "You are beyond redemption. You are beyond the pale. There's no hope for you"? If you did that, you've murdered them. Do you realise that if you ever think, much less say, of just a single soul, "They're beyond redemption", then you've murdered them because you've virtually destroyed the image of God in them and you have said, "You can't restore it now." You have taken a person, however low they have sunk, and you have taken an image of God that there is inside them – an image that needs to be restored and could be – and you've smashed it, and you are not going to try to restore it.

Now, frankly, when Jesus says that, this preacher is a murderer. So are most people. We stand as discovered murderers, not with weapons in our hands, but with weapons in our heads and in our hearts, and even on our tongues. If looks could kill, we have killed.

Jesus died on a cross, paying the supreme penalty of the law – capital punishment he accepted. A dying criminal beside him said, "We receive the due reward of our deeds." He recognised that this was right and just, as he was dying.

Jesus didn't say, "No, you're wrong, I've come to abolish capital punishment! This is a barbaric way of dealing with it!" Jesus said, "Today you'll be with me..." implying: you've accepted the justice, now I give you mercy. Jesus paid the supreme penalty that we murderers might go free. There was one murderer walking around Jerusalem's streets a day later — free, and his name was Barabbas. I am only alive today, and you are only alive today and enjoying this world, because we are like Barabbas. We can point at Jesus on the cross and say not only, "There but for the grace of God go I," but, "There by the grace of God went he."

James says in his letter, "You may have kept all the commandments, and yet just broken this one, 'thou shall not kill', and in doing so you've broken them all." Fancy choosing this one; you would have thought that somebody who kept all the others could keep this, that this is the least difficult to keep, but now we know it's not. Now we know that we have not always upheld the sanctity of life as we should, and that we have killed people in thought and word and feeling, even if we never have in deed.

7

No Adultery

Here is a rather sad and sordid story about the best king that Israel ever had.

In the spring of the following year, at the time when the wars begin, David sent Joab and the Israelite army to destroy the Ammonites. They began by laying siege to the city of Rabbah, but David stayed in Jerusalem. One night he couldn't get to sleep and went for a stroll on the roof of his palace. As he looked out over the city he noticed a woman of unusual beauty taking her evening bath. He sent to find out who she was and was told that she was Bathsheba, the daughter of Eliam and the wife of Uriah. Then David sent for her and when she came he slept with her. She had just completed the purification rites after menstruation. Then she returned home, and when she found that he had made her pregnant she sent a message to inform him. So David dispatched a memo to Joab, "Send me Uriah the Hittite."

When he arrived, David asked him how Joab and the army were getting along and how the war was prospering. Then he sent him to go home and relax, and he sent a present to him at his home but Uriah didn't go there. He stayed that night at the gateway of the palace with the other servants of the king. When David heard what Uriah had done he summoned him and asked him, "What's the matter with you? Why didn't you go home to your wife last night after you've been away for so long?"

Uriah replied, "The ark, and the armies, the general and his officers are camping out in open fields and should I go home to wine, dine, and sleep with my wife? I swear that I will never be guilty of acting like that."

"Well stay here tonight, and tomorrow you may return to the army." So Uriah stayed around the palace and David invited him to dinner and got him drunk, but even so he didn't go home that night but again he slept at the entry to the palace. Finally, the next morning David wrote a letter to Joab and gave it to Uriah to deliver. The letter instructed Joab to put Uriah at the front of the hottest part of the battle and then pull back and leave him there to die. So Joab assigned Uriah to a spot close to the besieged city where he knew that the enemy's best men were fighting, and Uriah was killed along with several other Israelite soldiers.

When Joab sent a report to David of how the battle was going he told his messenger, "If the king is angry and asks, 'Why did the troops go so close to the city? Didn't they know they would be shooting from the walls? Wasn't Abimelech killed at Thebez by a woman who threw down a millstone on him,' then tell him, 'Uriah was killed too.'"

So the messenger arrived at Jerusalem and gave the report to David, "The enemy came out against us," he said, "as we chased them back to the city gates the men on the wall attacked us and some of our men were killed, and Uriah the Hittite is dead too."

"Well, tell Joab not to be discouraged," David said. "The sword kills one as well as another. Fight harder next time and conquer the city. Tell him he's doing well."

When Bathsheba heard that her husband was dead, she mourned for him, and then when the period of mourning was over David sent for her and brought her to the palace and she became one of his wives and she gave birth to his son, but the Lord was very displeased with what David had done. So the Lord sent the prophet Nathan to tell David this story, "There were two men in a certain city, one very rich owning many flocks of sheep and herds of goats, the other very poor owning nothing but a little lamb he had managed to buy. It was his children's pet. He fed it from his own plate and let it drink from his own cup. He cuddled it in his arms like a baby daughter. Recently, a guest arrived at the home of the rich man, but instead of killing a lamb from his own flocks for food for the traveller, he took the poor man's lamb, and roasted it, and served it."

David was furious. "I swear by the living God," he vowed,

NO ADULTERY

"any man who would do a thing like that should be put to death.
He shall repay four lambs to the poor man for the one he stole
and for having no pity."

Then Nathan said to David, "You are that rich man. The Lord
God of Israel says, 'I made you king of Israel and saved you
from the power of Saul. I gave you his palace, and his wives,
and the kingdoms of Israel and Judah, and if that had not been
enough I would have given you much, much more. Why then
have you despised the laws of God and done this horrible deed?
For you have murdered Uriah and stolen his wife. Therefore
murder shall be a constant threat in your family from this
time on because you have insulted me by taking Uriah's wife.
I vow that because of what you have done I will cause your
own household to rebel against you. I will give your wives to
another man and he will go to bed with them in public view.
You did it secretly but I will do this to you openly in the sight
of all Israel.'"

"I have sinned against the Lord," David confessed to Nathan.

Then Nathan replied, "Yes, but the Lord has forgiven you and
you won't die for this sin. But you have given great opportunity
to the enemies of the Lord to despise and blaspheme him, so
your child shall die."

2 Samuel 11

During the Second World War, as the Russian armies drove forward
to meet the Americans and the British, a Mrs Burgmeier who was
out foraging for food for her children and herself was picked up.
Without being able to get any word to the children, she was taken
away to a prison camp in the Ukraine. Meanwhile, her husband
was captured and ended up in a prison camp in Wales. Ultimately
the husband was released. He went back to Germany, and after
weeks of searching he found the children, the two youngest in a
Russian detention school and the oldest hiding in a cellar. They
had no idea where their mother was. They never stopped searching
for her. They knew that only her return could ever knit that family
together again after all that had happened to them.

Meanwhile, away in the Ukraine a kindly camp commandant
told Mrs Bergmeier that her family were together again and that

they were trying to find her, but they could not release her, for release was only given for two reasons. First, a prisoner was released if he or she was suffering from disease with which the camp could not cope, and was in that case moved to a Russian hospital. Second, a woman was released if she became pregnant. In that case, women were returned to Germany as a liability and no use for work. Mrs Bergemeir thought it out and finally she decided to ask a friendly, vulgar, German camp guard to make her pregnant. He did. Her condition was medically verified; she was sent back to Germany and received with open arms by her family. She told them what she had done and they thoroughly approved. In due time the baby was born. They called him Dietrich, and they loved him most of all because they felt he had done more for them than any of the others. For the German guard they had nothing but a grateful and affectionate memory.

That's quite a story, isn't it? I mention it because I want to show that no matter what the commandments are, if you let your heart rule your head you can always find circumstances in which you can justify to yourself breaking the commandment. But the simple fact is that in spite of all the benefit of that whole experience and decision, she broke the seventh commandment deliberately, knowingly. There are many lesser circumstances today in which people justify the same action. More often it is justified on the grounds of love. We have reached a point in our society where people will say, "It is better for two people to live together who are not married if they love each other than for two people who are married to go on living together after they have stopped loving each other."

We live in a climate of opinion in which adultery is not considered anything terribly wrong provided it does not hurt anyone and provided there is true love behind it. This is the kind of climate in which Christianity first appeared in the Greek and Roman empire. I daresay if the Duke of Windsor had fallen in love with Mrs Wallis today, the country would have allowed him to remain on the throne. Certainly no eyebrows are raised when prominent people in our society start a relationship with others.

Why did God lay down this principle of no adultery? Is it yet another example, as the worldling would say, of God being narrow-minded, a spoilsport? Can he not feel that you may no longer love your married partner, and that you profoundly love someone else? Does not God understand, since he made us, what human love leads us to do? What is wrong with adultery? That may seem a strange question to ask Christians, because in these matters church opinion is usually well behind world opinion, though it is catching up fast. We have to look at this whole matter objectively and honestly. We may find that this law has something to say to most of us.

I want to speak about five reasons why God laid down this basic law, factors that he had in mind when he said, "Don't do it." I want to consider the significance of sex, the meaning of marriage, the level of love, the danger of divorce and the safeguarding of society. Here are five things, which I believe from the Bible to be in the mind of God as he said this thing.

First, *the significance of sex*. Every one of us has it and finds that it is bound up with total life – it is one of the most powerful urges in our make-up, and it's there. Now what exactly is it? The humanist would have us believe that it is no different from any other physical appetite, a desire of our body that should be satisfied. It is of the same order as the desire for food and drink. We are seen by the humanist as being basically animals, and sex a hangover from our animal evolutionary history. So it is thought that because it is simply a physical desire it must be satisfied at all costs and in any way. There is no moral difference between preferring the wife next door's cooking and Yorkshire pudding to preferring her attractions. Now here is a basic view of a simple physical appetite. But when I read the Bible I find two more things are said about this.

Firstly, that sex is not only a physical thing it is a psychic thing. I mean by this that a physical act of sex cannot be treated as the same thing as eating someone else's Yorkshire pudding for the simple reason that Yorkshire pudding does not involve your whole personality, whereas sex does. In giving yourself physically in this way, you are giving yourself "psychically" and you can never be the same again. You have given yourself to someone, not just physically but psychologically and emotionally. You are involved – not just your stomach but you as a person. You cannot separate this appetite from your total being—that's the biblical understanding.

Furthermore, the Bible indicates that this is not just a physical and a psychological thing, it is a spiritual part of us. That may come as news to you. But let me start in Genesis 1, where God says, "Let us make man in our image. So he made man in his own image, male and female made he them." As much as to say the fact that we are sexual beings is somehow reflecting spiritual things. That is why in the heart of the Bible there is a love song, which embarrasses many Christians by its erotic poetry. It's called the Song of Solomon.

We spiritualise it to get away from the simple fact that in the middle of the Bible is an erotic love song, but it is there because it does in fact correspond to something very deeply spiritual. Christians down the years have found in that love song the very expressions they wanted to use about their relationship to the Lord. Paul takes the same thing up in Ephesians 5 where he says that marriage is a picture of the relationship between Christ and the church. So sex is not just a physical appetite; it involves the whole person, and it is a spiritual thing. Therefore we come to our first basic principle: whenever we try to treat it as an isolated physical thing alone – simply as an appetite – then we rob it of its context and sooner or later we will spoil it.

The second thing I want to consider is *the meaning of marriage*. What exactly happens when two people marry? Is it simply a convenience that two can live as cheaply as one? That, by the way, is the biggest myth that has ever been! But is it simply that they are saying, "Well, let's combine forces. Let's cook for each other, sleep with each other, and that's much more convenient than trailing around from our house to your house." Is it just a convenience so that two people can look after each other and look after themselves better? Is it just a contract between two people who are agreeing to do certain things for each other for as long as they wish to and at any point when they feel they have had enough, the contract can be cancelled and they can walk out of it?

The answer of the Bible is that it is far more than a convenience, far more than a contract. Something absolutely radical changes in the lives of two people when they marry, and it is this: the two become one. Not just one flesh—though their bodies will be united – they become one *person*. Therefore if two have become one, then each one has become "half". I am only half a person now and my wife is my better half! As long as the spouse is alive, the other person remains half a person. One is incomplete without the other. There is only one thing in the Bible that restores wholeness to such a half person and that is death. It is mentioned in Mark 12 and in Romans 7, that death alone can restore wholeness to a person. Death does do that for the very simple reason that the body, through which sacramentally you became one person through one flesh, is no longer a body on earth. Therefore the marriage is broken and the wholeness has been restored to the half person. That is why in marriage services the couple say, "till death us do part". Even if they are two Christians looking forward to being in heaven together, we are stating very clearly that on earth the halfness will be restored to wholeness in the event of the death of the partner.

Here then is the meaning of marriage. If that is to take place, there must not only be a cleaving or a clinging between two people, there must be a leaving that has preceded that. "A man shall leave his father and mother and cleave to his wife." One relationship has to be broken in order that the other may be made.

So marriage is therefore never a private matter. It is not a thing that you can just have with two people deciding to live together. It affects other people; it affects society. I am sure that all of us who have been married had a stage just before the wedding where we wanted to get off to Gretna Green by ourselves and forget the rest. All the business of, "Shall we have auntie so and so," and all the rest and, "Who will be offended if we don't send an invitation?"

But it is right and proper that a marriage should be public for this reason: you are breaking other relationships to make this one. It is affecting others very deeply when two become one. For one thing, people are now related "in law" who were not related before. You now have a mother-in-law, and in law you have a father and the two families have been united. That is a meaning of marriage.

Thirdly, we consider *the level of love*. Everybody is singing about it, everybody is talking about it, everybody wants it, but what is it? How would you define "love"? One of our difficulties is that the English language is just so limited that we use one word for all the meanings, whereas the Greeks had a variety of words to use. Now there are three views of marriage and what love constitutes. I'm going to label them the rational view, the romantic view, and the religious view.

The rational view said that love is primarily a matter of the mind, and of deciding who fits whom, who is well matched, and of arranging the marriage. There was a time in many societies when marriages were arranged for children. It is still a formal tradition in some circles to ask her father if you can have her, It's a formality now but in older days it was a very serious business. The whole thing was gone into rationally.

"What are your prospects young man? Can you look after my daughter? Are you well matched? Do your temperaments go together?" A whole lot of questions were asked rationally. One thinks of the young man who said to his girl, "I'm making a list of your good points. I've got to fifteen, and when I get to twenty I'll ask you to marry me."

She said, "You'd better hurry up because I'm making a list of your bad points and I've got to nineteen." Now that is the rational approach to love.

I'm going to say that I believe many people are making a big mistake in ruling out a rational side to love. I have said to young people: if you really are well matched and meant for each other, others will feel so too, who don't have your feelings but who will rationally look at both of you and say, "They are well matched." It can be a very good check on your own guidance.

But now we've seen the swing from rational love to romantic love – the transfer of the understanding of love from the head to the heart and the interpretation of love entirely in terms of feeling. Now if our love has no feeling in it there's something wrong with it, but if it is entirely feeling and no more, then equally there's something wrong with it. But the false view of the romantic approach to love is this—that love stops as soon as you have no feelings for that person, love has vanished. That is the purely romantic view.

Now let me come to the Christian view, which is neither the rational nor the solely romantic. This view is that the heart of love rests not just in what you *think* about a person nor only how you *feel* about a person, but in the way you *act* towards them. It is centered therefore not just in the mind or heart, but also in the will. It has a rational understanding, it has a romantic feeling, but when a couple stands to be married and I stand in front of them, I do not say to them, "Do you think you are well matched? Do others think you are well matched? Do your parents approve?"

Nor do I say to them, "What are your feelings for each other at this moment?" They're usually fairly glassy-eyed and not fully with us, and their feelings really are not what they will be. But I don't ask them how they feel, and they do not reply to my questions, "I think I love this person." Nor do they say, "I feel I love this person." I say, "How are you going to act towards them? Are you prepared to be loyal whatever happens? For better, for worse, for richer, for poorer, in sickness and in health? Are you prepared to act towards them in loyalty?"

If so, then that is true love in God's sight because that is the kind of love that God has for us. It is not a love that is conditioned by what he thinks of us, and we know what he may think of us. It is not a love primarily conditioned by what he feels about us because I think there must be times when he has very mixed feelings about us. It is the kind of love that says, "I will. I love you for better, for worse. I've taken you to be my own." Jesus, having loved his own, loved them to the end in spite of what they did.

So love need not stop when feeling vanishes. Nor need love stop when mentally and rationally every argument points to breaking the thing up. Love could still go on if it is the view of love as portrayed in the Bible.

My fourth point is about *the danger of divorce*. It is a problem that is pressing right into Christian congregations now, and it is a problem that I have had to deal with again and again. (For a more detailed examination of this matter, see my book entitled *Remarriage is Adultery Unless*....) In brief, what does the Bible say about divorce? Again it is vital to be ruled by the Word rather than the world, and by the head rather than the heart. I'm going to ask three questions, which are delicate ones for many: What does God think about divorce? Are there not times when separation is the lesser of two evils? Does that make remarriage possible?

First, what does God think about divorce? There is no doubt whatever about the answer. In Malachi 2:16, God says, "I hate divorce." Nothing could be clearer and there is no question that Jesus disliked it intensely and reflected his Father's attitude. So there is a simple answer to the first question. It is alien to God's plan for his people. It is not a thing that God wanted to happen or intended to happen. I wish the answer to the other two questions were as simple.

The second question: are there not times when separation is

the lesser of two evils? The answer of the Bible is: yes, there are times when this is the right step to take, not because it is a good step but because it is a less bad step. The situation that the New Testament envisages is where the home has reached such a point that the God who is harmony and peace is no longer reflected in the situation and children are being brought up in a situation of constant antagonism, hatred, and fighting. The New Testament does seem to say quite clearly that there are times when this is, alas, necessary and it were better for two people to live separately than to go on living a cat and dog existence together.

There is a special case also mentioned in 1 Corinthians 7, and an unusual one but a common one. It is this—where a couple have married and later after their marriage one of them has become a Christian. This is a real source of tension and frustration between the two. I have known many homes where this has happened. What was a peaceful home with two unbelievers becomes a profoundly unhappy home because there is now an unequal yoke. The Bible teaches that one must never enter that unequal yoke if one is a Christian before marrying; a Christian can only marry a Christian. But many are converted after marrying, and it causes real friction. Here Paul states quite clearly this principle, as far as the Christian partner is concerned: they should stay with the marriage as long as they can in the hope of leading their partner to Christ. "Who knows whether the wife will save her husband or the husband her wife," says Paul.

But the other side to it is this—if the unbeliever desires to go the Christian should let them and is not bound to stay with them. The reason is that in a sense the partner's conversion has been a bit unfair to the unbeliever. He did not marry a Christian. He had no intention of marrying a Christian. If that partner had been a Christian when they were courting, that would have been the end of it. Suddenly now he's married to a Christian and that is an embarrassing situation.

One of the most humorous verses in the Bible, which I've never preached on because I don't think I could keep a straight face is after Jacob's first marriage and: "Lo, in the morning behold it was Leah," which seems to me the most masterly understatement in the entire Bible. He thought he had Rachel. In the same way, unbelieving husbands, or more rarely wives, have suddenly woken up to the fact that they are married to a different person to the one who stood in the service with them. Paul says if the unbelieving partner wants to be out, let them go because God is a God of harmony and he doesn't want disharmony in his name. There are situations in which a separation is the lesser of two evils and a good thing, relatively.

Now we come to the third and most difficult question, the heart of the problem and it needs great honesty: does separation allow remarriage? We must keep these matters separate. I wish we could because divorce has put them too close together. For a married couple to separate is one thing, and for either partner to remarry is another. But people take divorce as permission to remarry. This verse sets the tone: "A wife must not leave her husband, but if she is separated from him let her remain single or else go back to him." Here is the situation envisaged where it does become necessary for the sake of peace to have separation. It is quite clear, where that happens: let the partner remain single or be reconciled to the one they have left. That is the basic position of the New Testament. Is there any exception to it?

I come now to something Jesus himself said when he was asked about the question of divorce. There was a great debate going on in his day about divorce. Two rabbis, Shammai and Hillel, taught different interpretations of God's Word. Moses had said that if a man marries a wife and finds some unclean thing in her he may write a bill of divorce and separate, and be free to remarry. The debate was what is meant by "some unclean thing". Shammai said only one thing: adultery. Hillel said that an unclean thing can cover a whole lot of things. It can mean burning your toast at breakfast, over salting the soup, talking loudly, or going out of doors with her head uncovered – or even your meeting a more attractive woman. You can guess which rabbi was the more popular preacher.

Jesus was asked which of those two interpretations he as a teacher adopted. His answer meant neither of those. He said, "Whoever divorces his wife except for the cause of fornication and marries another commits adultery."

Notice he says "fornication". Many people have overlooked that, and have gained the general impression that Jesus made adultery the one exception. What did he mean? I can only pass on to you the result of my own study in this. I went through this because I was asked to prepare a paper for the divorce reform group made up of Members of Parliament and ministers of the church before the reform of the divorce laws.

I made this discovery: "adultery" is always used for the wrong or illicit sex relationship by a married person with someone other than their partner whereas "fornication" is always used of a wrong sex relationship by a single person, and these two things are listed alongside each other as different terms. What is Jesus meaning when he talks about divorcing your partner on the ground of fornication? The answer is that he is not referring to something that has happened since the marriage but something that happened when they were still single and had not been disclosed at the time of the wedding. That is a very narrow exception and, oddly enough, is not a ground for divorce in English law. Jesus is referring to undisclosed infidelity before the marriage, so the person who came to the marriage was only half a person at the beginning and had already been one with someone else, and this had not been disclosed, therefore not forgiven before the marriage, so the marriage had not set off on the right foot.

If that is what Jesus is saying, a number of things would confirm it. First, Moses had said, "If a man marries a woman and he finds some unclean thing in her he can divorce her unless her parents can bring proof of her virginity," so Jesus is not correcting Moses but agreeing. The next argument that would indicate that this is the right interpretation is the disciples' extraordinary reaction to his ruling. Their reaction amounted to this: If that is so, you can never get divorced at all. There's no point in getting married. You could never get out of it. They saw Jesus' words as ruling divorce out of court.

This in fact was the very ground on which Jesus nearly had divorce in his own family circle, because it was before Joseph and Mary were married that Joseph discovered she was with child, and being a just man resolved to divorce her on the ground of Moses' law. Jesus is now referring to exactly the same thing. In other words, the only ground for breaking up a marriage is that it never got started, which makes sense. It is rational and you can understand why Jesus makes that point. Jesus went on to correct the disciples' view. If I am right in interpreting Jesus' words, then all the grounds of modern divorce fall to the ground.

Jesus is saying that remarriage after divorce is adultery. Search the scriptures for yourself and find out if these things are so. What we cannot do is to go against the teaching of Christ if we profess to belong to him. Every one of us must follow our own conscience and understanding on this.

Fifth, and finally, we turn to *the safeguarding of society*. What a brick is to the building, a marriage is to the community. There can be no doubt that a society will crumble and collapse if marriage collapses. History is strewn with this kind of story. I mention only the Roman Empire. For the first five hundred years of the Roman commonwealth there is no record of a marriage breaking up. Then Rome conquered Greece, and Greece conquered them. One of the greatest Greek philosophers said, "We have courtesans for pleasure, concubines for cohabitation, and wives to have our children and keep our house." That was treated as normal and natural. Cicero and Socrates upheld this system. They had mistresses as well as wives, and you could divorce your wife without any legal proceedings by simply telling her in front of two witnesses, "Go." Rome conquered Greece, the morals of Greece spread, and from that day we have the beginnings of the first records of marriage break up, until in Rome itself marriage became a thing of the past. It is recorded that one woman had eight husbands in five years shortly after Rome conquered Greece. By the time of our Lord, children were simply a nuisance, because when you came to divorce they were in the way, and morals slid down. The Roman empire did not crack up because it was attacked from outside but because the bricks of its society crumbled within. When a sufficient number of bricks crumble, the house falls.

God's command, "No adultery" is saying something essential just to keep society going. Marriage is the cement of society. If you in your home today are holding together a marriage by the kind of love that says, "I will", you are doing something great for this nation.

I have made my five points, but it may well be that most who read this are feeling fairly comfortable still, and maybe we shouldn't be, because Jesus does something to the Ten Commandments as he draws out their implications. What he did with the sixth he does with the seventh. With the sixth he made it clear that murder is not just what you do with your hand but what you do with your heart. With the seventh he does the same thing: adultery begins inside not outside, and that is where it starts. He points to the spirit rather than only the letter of the law. We face the pressures that are on us in society to be unfaithful and to look elsewhere. Jesus impresses on us that we are to fight the battle *inside* and win it there.

The New Testament goes on beyond mental adultery and emotional adultery to talk of spiritual adultery. That is described in these terms: if you love God and you love the world as well, that is spiritual adultery. The law is widened out in the New Testament to cover far more than the physical act. It covers the mental thought and it covers spiritual infidelity to the one who loves us and who married us in Christ. That finds most of us out, as the law does. Paul points out that it is by the straight edge of the law that we see how crooked we are.

But this sin is not, and never will be, the unforgivable sin. In the Old Testament we read of Hosea, a preacher who married a prostitute. It didn't work out and she went back to her old way of life. Hosea found in his heart a love that went looking for her in the marketplace, found her, brought her back home, and loved her and forgave her. Through that experience Hosea came to know the forgiveness that God has, and the grace of God that says: I have loved you freely. I will heal your backslidings.

Jesus said to a woman caught in the very act. "Go and sin no more, neither do I condemn you." It is not the unforgiveable sin but it is still sin. All of us have within us the capacity to be unfaithful.

8

Do Not Steal

As Jesus was passing through Jericho, a man named Zacchaeus, one of the most influential Jews in the Roman tax collecting business, and of course a very rich man, tried to get a look at Jesus but he was too short to see over the crowds. So he ran ahead and climbed into a sycamore tree beside the road to watch from there. When Jesus came by he looked up at Zacchaeus and called him by name, "Zacchaeus," he said, "Quick, come down for I'm going to be a guest in your home today." Zacchaeus hurriedly climbed down and took Jesus to his house in great excitement and joy, but the crowds were displeased.

"He has gone to be the guest of a notorious sinner," they grumbled.

Meanwhile Zacchaeus stood before the Lord and said, "Sir, from now on I will give half my wealth to the poor and if I find I have overcharged anyone on his taxes I will penalise myself by giving him back four times as much."

Jesus told him, "This shows that salvation has come to this home today."

Luke 19:1–9a

Two others, criminals, were led out to be executed with him at a place called, "The Skull". There all three were crucified, Jesus on the centre cross and the two criminals on either side. "Father forgive these people," Jesus said, "For they don't know what they are doing."

The soldiers gambled for his clothing, throwing dice for

each piece, and the crowd watched. The Jewish leaders laughed and scoffed. "He was so good at helping others," they said, "Let's see him save himself if he really is God's chosen one, the Messiah."

The soldiers mocked him too by offering him a drink of sour wine. They called to him, "If you are the King of the Jews save yourself!" A signboard was nailed to the cross above him with these words, "This is the King of the Jews."

One of the criminals hanging beside him scoffed, "So you're the Messiah are you? Prove it by saving yourself and us too while you're at it."

But the other criminal protested, "Don't you even fear God when you are dying? We deserve to die for our evil deeds but this man hasn't done one thing wrong." Then he said, "Jesus remember me when you come into your kingdom."

Jesus replied, "Today you will be with me in Paradise. This is a solemn promise."

By now it was noon and the darkness fell across the whole land for three hours until three o'clock. The light from the sun was gone and suddenly the thick veil hanging in the Temple split apart. Then Jesus shouted, "Father, I commit my Spirit to you." With those words he died.

When the captain of the Roman military unit handling the executions saw what had happened he was stricken with awe before God and said, "Surely this man was innocent."

Luke 23:32ff.

An Indian boy brought up in a Christian mission came to this country as a student. The missionary who saw him off from India warned him that England was not such a Christian country as he might imagine, and that he would see many things here to disturb him. The lad came for three years, then went back and the same missionary met him and said, "Well, was it terribly disappointing?"

He said, "No, it was marvellous. On my first day in London I saw three miracles."

"Tell me more," the missionary replied.

"Well," he said, "I got a London bus and there was a lady sitting next to me and she got up to get off the bus but the conductor was nowhere in sight. He was upstairs on the upper deck. So the lady gave her bus fare to a man who had been sitting next to her to give to the conductor, miracle number one. The conductor came downstairs and the man gave him the fare, miracle number two. The conductor put it in the bag and punched a ticket for it, miracle number three." The only sad part of that story is that it happened over fifty years ago. I daresay an Indian visiting London today might not see quite so many miracles!

There was a newspaper report some years ago of a family of twenty who have been living for many years by theft alone. Their children had been brought up to steal. It was described in the press as a "pagan household". Of course, people hold up their hands in horror at such a thing. At least some do. But *why* is it wrong? If they needed it, why not take it? I have identified seven conditions, which others have suggested as supposedly excusing stealing today.

First: that you really need what you have stolen. That seems to be one rule that people live by. If you need it, it is thought by many to be all right to steal it. You have a right to live as everybody else has and therefore you have a right to what you need.

Secondly, it is thought that you have a right to steal it if the owner doesn't need it. Have you heard that said at the office? "Oh, that's never used. You might as well have it. It will come in useful at your home."

A third "condition" is you can steal it if the owner won't miss it.

A fourth appears to be that you can steal if the owner can afford to buy another. After all, he's got plenty of cash. He can soon get another, you can't.

Fifthly, you can steal provided it's on a small scale. As long as it's nothing big it is supposed to be all right.

Sixthly, you can steal provided it's not from someone you know. I don't know why that makes it all right but I've heard it said – because it really would be an act of betrayal to a friend, but of an enemy, it serves him right. A variant on this one is that provided you are not stealing from an individual but from a corporate body, that is all right. I am old enough to remember when they nationalised the coalmines and great big notices went up, which read, "This pit belongs to you" – and they took it literally.

There are those who have thought that the best way to stop stealing is to abolish private property. But it is amazing how many people think that provided you are stealing from some big body, and not from an individual, it is all right.

The seventh that I have come across is that it's all right to steal provided you can get away with it – "Thou shalt not be found out."

There are those, as I have pointed out, who say that the real problem is having property, and that if we were all sharing everything there would be no stealing. Don't you believe it. Communists did believe that a fully shared society in which everything was owned by the proletariat would not need any police for crime would disappear and stealing be a thing of the past. Historically, there have been at least seventy different attempts to abolish private property, and only five of them lasted more than four years.

We have in the eighth commandment a principle of the sanctity of property. In the sixth commandment we saw the sanctity of life, in the seventh commandment the sanctity of marriage, and we will come to the sanctity of reputation. But now we look at the eighth commandment which, among other things, means quite simply that there is nothing wrong with owning property.

Even communist societies have found fairly soon that people have property of one kind or another. It is not the fact that we have private property that causes stealing – it is something wrong with human nature, not the system. The New Testament never advocates practising communism. I know some people claim that it does. I will come back to that, but the difference between what they did in the New Testament and has been done in the name of communism is that in the New Testament it was voluntary and in the New Testament it was never total. A person could share what they wished – they could keep some for themselves and share some, it was not total.

The commandment is blunt, it is bold, it has no qualifications. It doesn't list a lot of circumstances in which stealing is all right. It just says don't do it.

We have observed that in every building site, every department store, every depot, there is what is euphemistically called "shrinkage". I could have shown you in our church building two doors which would have to be replaced. They were not the quality we had ordered. Why? Because five lovely birch doors one day walked from the site. So we had poorer quality ones put in temporarily until we could get the good ones installed. That very building had marks on it of the breaking of this commandment. We couldn't even construct a church building without it happening. Though the level of theft was remarkably little considering the lack of a fence around the building site. We prayed about this and it was kept well down.

Millions of pounds every year have to be allowed for stealing. Now there are two sorts of stealing I want to speak about: stealing from people and stealing from God. Those of us who may not have done much stealing from people need to remember the second part too: you can steal from God.

Let's look first at stealing from people. Why is it wrong? Well you could say, "Because God says so" – that is a simple answer but it's not quite enough, is it? Why does God say it? Why is it wrong? The answer is that it is against the laws of honest gain. There are two such laws: labour and love. You must either gain what you have through earnings or through gifts. These are the two honest ways of gaining anything. Other ways are not honest. The main source of income is to be labour for all of us.

Here are two texts, written by Paul, which are so down-to-earth that some people might think they came from a trade union manual rather than the Bible: *If any will not work, let him not eat.* That's the New Testament speaking and it is pretty blunt. Here is another: *Let the thief no longer steal but rather let him labour, doing honest work with his hands* [Notice that: using his hands in a different way] *so that he may be able to give to those in need.*

From these two texts one gets two things about the outlook of a thief which are bound to affect his character. Firstly, he is living to "get" rather than to give. Paul says let him stop stealing and work hard so that he can learn to give. Stealing will produce a *getting* kind of person, working hard will produce a *working hard* kind of person. The second thing is that he is trying to get something for nothing, trying to cut corners, trying to get rich quick, trying to avoid the exchange of goods or services that is a legitimate way of gain. A person who is a thief becomes a *something-for-nothing* kind of person.

Now when we have said those two things you realise that there are many ways of stealing. We don't like the word so we dress it up. We can call it "business acumen". We can call it all kinds of things, but let's look at some of the ways in which we could be stealing, living to get rather than to give and trying to get something for nothing. Plain *thieving* is the most obvious: the bank robber, the car thief, the safe breaker, the cat burglar. That clearly comes under this commandment. We don't need to argue about that, so I'm not going to. The most common form is perhaps shoplifting, mentioned earlier.

The second way is *cheating*: underpaying, overcharging, and grossly misleading advertising. At least we now have the Trade Descriptions Act, which my children wanted me to invoke. I would buy them some weekly sweets and I came home one week and said, "I've solved a problem in our family life." I had bought three long strips of toffee and it said on it, "Everlasting toffee". So I said, "Make the most of this, it is the last time I bring home some weekly sweets." Their reaction was to say, "Daddy, Trade Descriptions Act" – because it lasted about fifteen minutes.

At least we are aware that cheating is stealing, and we ought to call it that, whether it is getting off the bus without paying our fare, or bribing an official, or rigging a contract, or playing tricks with foreign exchange. An employer who does not give a fair day's wage, or an employee who does not give a fair day's work is cheating, which is stealing.

Thirdly, *exploiting*. During the war we had what was called the black market. Things were scarce so there was an underground market and you could buy some butter using it, you could buy some bacon – but you paid very highly because of the shortage. Some people made a great deal of money that way. I find myself constantly asking how near present house prices are coming to stealing in the sense of exploiting shortage. One just wonders how much further they can go before we are in fact in the realm of stealing in the form of exploitation. Scripture forbids usury among the poor. It forbids you to take advantage of a poor person by charging a high rate of interest. Perhaps that needs looking at in the light of our housing situation and mortgage facilities for a young couple struggling to get a home of their own.

Fourthly, we can steal by *gambling*. I will briefly mention what a gamble is. People say stock exchange trading is a gamble. It sometimes is, but it isn't of itself. Some people say insurance is a gamble. No, it's not. Gambling is *creating a risk of loss that did not exist before.* Insurance never does that; it deals with existing risks. Secondly, it is always trying to gain at someone else's loss and expense. How you can love your neighbor and try to do that I just don't understand. Thirdly, it is trying to get something for nothing, with no intention of exchanging any goods or values for the money received. Those three factors, when they are all present, constitute a gamble, whether it's a raffle ticket or five thousand pounds on the Derby winner. The size of stake does not matter in the slightest. Though gambling is not specifically dealt with in the Bible (except perhaps in the account of what took place among some of those present at the crucifixion), I believe we could say that a gambler is stealing.

Fifthly, *pilfering.* We used to be called a nation of shopkeepers, now we are a nation of shoplifters. Just little things maybe: hotel coat hangers, café teaspoons, cutlery, crockery, ashtrays, pencils and so on. I have only preached rarely on this commandment, and when I did on one occasion there was a man taking notes of the sermon in a notebook that he had "lifted" from the office. He got all the sermon down and then came to me afterwards with a major problem. What should he do? He didn't want to put it back in case they read it! The Bible would just call pilfering stealing.

Sixthly, there is *stealing by finding.* "Finding is keeping." Is it? Who said it was? I remember the day when, as a boy, I found a purse full of money. There it was on the pavement and I took it home with great glee. I was saving up for something and there was the money. But mother said, "The police station is at the top of the road."

Seventh, there is *"borrowing"*. If it is borrowing without asking or without returning, is it any different from stealing? The libraries of Britain have lost millions of books through such "borrowing". Not to pay a bill is actually forcing someone to lend you money. In the southern states of America there was a Negro preacher really warming up to this theme. He said, "All members of the congregation who have been stealing chicken stand to your feet and confess." Nobody moved. "All members of the congregation who've been stealing piglets, stand to your feet and confess." Again nobody moved. "All members of the congregation who've been stealing corn, stand to your feet and confess." Still nobody moved.

So he closed the sermon, they had the last hymn, he stood at the door, and as they went out one man, wiping his brow, said, "Pastor, if you'd said 'ducks' I'd have been a goner." Which reminds us that the Lord has his own way of finding us out. We may not have touched specifically on something in your life or mine, but that doesn't mean that God's law doesn't apply. The Holy Spirit will apply it in his way.

The other story from the same area was a group of deacons who took the pastor into the vestry after a sermon on this commandment and said to the pastor, "Now pastor, you stick to the gospel and keep off chicken stealing." But the pastor was right – the gospel is concerned with chicken stealing because the gospel is about salvation. When a man called Zacchaeus said, "I'm going to pay back four-fold," Jesus said, "Salvation has got here." Salvation has come if it shows like that.

There is another form of stealing in the Bible which we must look at, and it is *stealing from God*. What an extraordinary phrase! Of course, if stealing were all right, if you can take something from someone who can afford it, then you can steal from God. He has got everything. But let's look a little more closely at this phrase. If stealing from men shows you have a wrong attitude to other people's property, stealing from God shows you have a wrong attitude to your own property. I'll explain that in a moment. To say, "What's thine is mine" is stealing from men. But to say, "What's mine is my own" is stealing from God, according to the Bible.

Let's go back to New Testament "communism". It does say in Acts 4:32 that not one of the early Christians said that anything he possessed was his own. People have jumped to the conclusion that therefore what they said was, "It isn't mine, it's yours." That is not what they said. What they said was, "It isn't mine, it's his" – and that is a totally different thing. They believed that when the Lord Jesus paid such a price with his own blood, he not only bought me, he bought everything I have too. That is a profound understanding of the redemption that Christ came to bring. He not only bought me, he bought me out and bought everything I have got. Therefore it's not mine, it's his. "Render to God the things that are God's."

Let us look at three ways in which we could rob God. First, we can rob God of *money*. When you put something in the collection plate, did you think that you were giving him something of yours, or did you not rather see that you were giving him something of his? What a huge difference that makes to the collection. Second, we can rob God in *time*. How much of God's work is stunted and held back because of one little phrase: "I haven't time." Yet we all have all the time there is. Every one of us has twenty-four hours a day. We may not be equal in terms of the money we have, but he has given us equal time. We can rob God of time that he should have had because it is *his*. It is not just that when I am in church that's his time, it's not even that Sunday is his time – the real Christian understanding is that he bought me so he bought all my time. The question is how much of his time am I allowed to have, not: how much of my time is *he* going to get?

The third way in which we can rob God terribly is of our *gifts*. I do not believe there is a single Christian without a gift. There are some with more gifts than others, and God sovereignly distributes them, but the Bible says he distributes gifts to each. Everybody has a gift to use. It may be significant that the man with one talent was the man who buried in a napkin and he produced it later, and the master was wrathful with that servant because he said: you've robbed me in not using the gift I left with you. You have no interest – you could have put it out to usury; you could have invested it. I could have had something out of it. Instead, because you only had one little gift you buried it, and you have robbed me of the interest. If God has invested gifts in us it is because he was looking for interest from those gifts. If I say, "I haven't got a gift", or if I say, "I'm sorry, I am too busy for my gift to be available", then I am robbing God.

It is important to mention that *there is forgiveness available for stealing*. It is not the unforgivable sin. If you've been brought up respectably, you may look down on a shoplifter or somebody in a factory who pinches tools but I want to say there can be forgivenes. I prove that by a dying thief who in the last minute of his life, paying for his deeds said, "Lord..." and the Lord forgave him.

Finally – why would we steal when we are so rich? I have heard of a young man from a wealthy home, who was shoplifting. That's mad, yet some do it. Why should we Christians think of "getting" when we are like millionaires – we live in Christ, and through his poverty we have become rich. All things are ours in Christ. The whole universe is to be ours, so let's live like millionaires. Let us realise that we are here to give, to dispense the riches of God's grace – not to be taking from other people, not to be trying to win competitions, not to be trying to get something for nothing, but here to dispense the wealth of our heavenly Father. That is our privilege. Let him who steals steal no more, but rather let him do honest work with his hands, that he may have, to give to those in need.

9

No False Witness

The ninth commandment of God through Moses is, "You shall not bear false witness." The more we study the Ten Commandments, the more one sees there are not ten but one. These Ten Commandments are like the links in a chain: break any one of the links and you have broken the whole chain. The New Testament shows us this, so you should consider the standard of your life not by the strongest link but the weakest – not by those commandments of God you have managed to keep, but those you break. We see the Ten Commandments as a whole standard of life – it is certainly not as if God added at the bottom that we need only attempt six out of ten. But this is his chain of Christian character; this is his chain of morality. If we break it at any point, we have rendered the whole useless; we have broken the law. It is said that we come in the ninth commandment to one that is broken more widely and more frequently than any of the other nine, so here is a weak link in the chain for many of us.

There are two ways in which the ninth commandment is linked very closely to some of the others. One way is that the last three commandments – numbers eight, nine, and ten – are all concerned with robbery. Number eight talks about robbing someone in deed, number nine robbing them in word, number ten robbing them in thought: "Thou shalt not covet." We can also link this commandment with one of the others. We saw that there are five concerned with our relationship to God, five with our relationship to men, and in each of those five one of the five – the third and the ninth – are concerned with the tongue.

The most deadly weapon a Roman soldier possessed was a short, wide sword with a spine down the middle, and it was the exact shape and appearance of a tongue. This is why, in scripture, words are often described in terms of a two-edged sword. As the Roman soldier could take a piece of steel shaped like a tongue and do damage with it, so we can do the same thing. The very term "cutting remark" indicates this.

Now here we come to the ninth commandment, concerned with what we say. We are going to find that in spite of its more limited application to perjury in court, there is a wider sense in which all of us have to listen to this commandment and let its sharp edge penetrate very deep. How serious are sins of the tongue? Most of us excuse them and treat them lightly. There's a little jingle we used to know as children which went something like this, "Sticks and stones may hurt my bones, but names will never hurt me." If ever there was an untruth, that is it. Shakespeare was much nearer the mark when he said, "Who steals my purse steals trash, but he that filches from me my good name robs me of that which not enriches him and makes me poor indeed." That is very much nearer the true position.

The Bible takes this very seriously. You have heard of the *lex talionis*, the law which states, "An eye for an eye, a tooth for a tooth, and a life for a life." That law, a very profound example of justice, was such a severe punishment that it was reserved in the Jewish law for only three crimes, one of which was perjury. If a man bearing false witness in a court caused another innocent person to suffer, then he should be made to suffer in exactly the same way, and in the same proportion: an eye for an eye, and a tooth for a tooth.

In the New Testament, sins of the tongue are taken even more seriously. Here are the words of Jesus, "And I tell you this, that you must give account on Judgment Day for every idle word you speak." Your words now reflect your fate then. Either you will be justified by them or you will be condemned by them. Few things have been said that are as serious as that. "Every idle word." Consider the teaching of Paul. In the same breath he classes slanderers with murderers and says neither shall inherit the kingdom of God. So slanderers and murderers are put in exactly the same bracket. Here, then, is the crime, sin, vice – call it what you will – with which the ninth commandment deals.

Now why does the Bible take this so seriously? The answer is that justice becomes impossible without truth. Why does a court spend so long hearing so many witnesses? I have sat through many tedious hours in court and thought what a wearisome business it is, day after day. Why do they do it? The answer is because justice cannot be done until the truth has been discovered. Therefore when a person is put in the dock they take a Bible in their hand and say, "I swear by Almighty God to tell the truth, the whole truth, and nothing but the truth" or they make an Affirmation. Until that is done, justice is hindered. Lies cause the guilty to go free and the innocent to suffer. Lies pervert justice, and it is because God is a God of justice that he demands truth. To be untrue about another is to cause unfair things to happen. Justice and truth belong together.

Now let's ask three questions. First of all, what is the sin that God is thinking of? Secondly, how do we commit it? Thirdly, why do we do it? Every one of us, I think, has to ask why we have done it – because we have. What has made us do this thing?

First of all, then, what is it? We'll begin with its proper basic meaning of perjury, which occurs in a court of law. Perjury is that crime of standing in the witness box and not telling the truth. It is one of the most serious crimes in English law. It is taken very seriously because it perverts the cause of justice. Now I want you to notice that it is not enough to say things that are true. A false witness may say things that are true, but it may not be the *whole* truth.

There are two ways of perverting truth. One is to tell less than the whole truth and the other is to tell more than the whole truth. Either way is false witness and perjury. It is not just enough that what you say about others is true in itself, we need to say the whole truth, give the whole picture – and we need to not add a single detail to it. "I swear by Almighty God to tell the truth" – that's not enough. "The whole truth" means I won't hold things back. "Nothing but the truth" means that I won't embellish with my own impressions, opinions, or imaginations. So there is the crime of perjury. Few of us have found ourselves in a witness box in court, and therefore we have not been tempted to withhold the truth or add to it in a legal case. Therefore we may be feeling comfortable at the moment, but let's go a little further.

There is another court, in which all of us are witnesses, and it is the court of public opinion. The only way you can avoid getting into the witness box in that court is never to open your mouth and talk about anyone else. If you do that then you will cut yourself off and live the life of a hermit. Every one of us has talked about other people, and witnessed to them in the court of public opinion. What we have said has determined whether they have been treated fairly or unfairly by those to whom we have spoken. Every one us has been in that witness box.

The word "gossip" has an interesting history. If I called you a "gossip", how would you feel? Would you speak to me again? If I said it five hundred years ago you would have been thrilled, counting it as a compliment, but not now. The word "gossip" originally had a "d" in it. The word originally was "god-ship" – and it meant a godly interest in other people, a prayerful concern for them. When godparents came to a child's christening they were asked, "Are you willing to be godships for this baby?" Then it became "gossip", so a gossip was somebody who would gossip to God about someone else and pray for them.

Then it declined and it became a word meaning a friendly interest. In Shakespeare's *Henry V*, there is a scene the night before the battle of Agincourt when two soldiers are talking to each other and saying how friendly they are, in case they are both killed the next day, and they describe each other not as pals or as buddies but, "You're my gossip," meaning "you're my pal". But the meaning has changed. There are two quotes I use: George MacDonald said, "Gossip is a beast of prey that does not wait for the death of the creature it devours"; Pascal said, "If everyone in the world knew what everyone said about the other, there would not be left four friends in the world."

It is a sobering thought that hardly anyone would be happy to have everything they have said about someone else told to them. This is the way in which we break the ninth commandment.

So how do we bear false witness? I have given some clues already. You can of course just tell a downright lie you have made up about somebody. Not many of us do that – I think we see it for what it is. Perhaps the nearest we get is to pass on a rumour without checking whether it is true, which is very close.

But there are more subtle ways in which we break this commandment. Here are four simple ones. By selection of the truth – and I mean just passing on some details but not the whole.

As I have mentioned already, you can create a false impression. A downright lie is not nearly as dangerous as a half-truth. The second way in which we may have done it is by suggestion. We don't say anything, we just hint. We sort of say, "Well if nothing fishy is going on, why does he spend so much time at her house?" That's the kind of thing. You see, there is just a hint and a suggestion. You haven't uttered a downright lie, you have just asked a question and you have sown a seed. The third thing is silence: to let a story you know to be untrue go unchallenged. A fourth way of bearing false witness is by stretching the truth if it serves your end to do so, adding details that were not in what you received.

Two further comments are relevant. First, even if the story is true, that does not necessarily mean that it is right to pass it on. The Bible teaches that if it is true the person to pass it on to is the person concerned, not someone else. In other words, say it to their face and not behind their back. The other thing to mention is that you can be a false witness *for* somebody as opposed to being a false witness against them. Flattery is being a false witness for someone. From time to time I'm asked, because of my position, to give a reference for somebody, it being supposed that a minister of religion's reference is of some value. I heard one businessman say it wasn't, because it would invariably be too optimistic and just say nice things. I'm afraid I'm warning you now that if you want a reference I will give you an honest one because I think a reference ought to be honest. You can be a false witness for someone by covering something up – as well as against them, exaggerating the fault.

Why do we do it? Why do we find ourselves bearing false witness about others in the court of public opinion? It is amazing how easy we find it. There is something horrible here. All of us find it only too easy. Trying to read my own and others' hearts, here are four reasons. The first is cowardice. Sometimes people bear false testimony in court because they are afraid of telling the truth. There are people who know things about their neighbours and they are afraid to tell. They are afraid to go to the authorities for fear of reprisal. Cowardice can prevent us from telling the whole truth. We are afraid of what would happen if we told the whole truth and nothing but the truth.

The second reason is prejudice. If we have come to an opinion and the facts do not fit our opinion then we tend, if we are not careful, to twist the facts to fit our opinion. It is one of the foibles of our human mind that we can do this. As one lady said to another about a third, "I don't like her, and from all I've said about her I never will," which is quite a remark. If we have come to a prejudiced conviction, and then the report reaches us which does not fit in with what we have already decided, then we are tempted to be false witnesses.

The third reason is avarice. Sometimes we can gain something. Two of you in the office are up for promotion. What a temptation it is to spread something about the other candidate that might get back to the boss, and might prejudice him in your favour.

The fourth reason, however, is the main one: malice. The hard fact is that we enjoy it, and we enjoy gossip. If we didn't enjoy it, three-quarters of the newspapers published today would go out of business. The problem is that if you enjoy taking it in through the eye or the ear, you cannot deny yourself the pleasure of letting it come out of the mouth. That is a law of human nature. What goes into a person comes out. Where did we get this from? Quite simply you got it from your father. So did I. Not my earthly father, nor my heavenly Father, my other one. Jesus on one occasion said to a group of men: "You are of your father the devil. He is the father of lies." That's where we got it from; that's why we do it. Go back to the beginning of the Bible, and you find from the very beginning that the devil, far from telling downright lies, twisted the truth round so that it sounded like the truth but was not—that is his nature. He came to Adam and Eve in the garden and said to Eve, "Has God told you not to eat any of the trees of the garden?" There was only one word there that was different from what God had said, but it twisted the whole meaning. God had said, "You shall not eat of the fruit of one tree in the garden." Notice that later the devil again told a half-truth. He said, "If you take this fruit your eyes will be opened and you will be like gods" – and that was half true. They took the fruit and their eyes were opened and they were like animals.

This is the devil's twisted mind – that he doesn't tell a downright lie, he tells a half-truth; he twists one word. You notice that because the devil did it, and because Adam and Eve submitted to the devil, they and their children got the same habit of twisting the truth. God said, "Adam, where are you?" and Adam said that he was naked. Is that why he was hiding? That was only half the truth. Yes he was naked and he was embarrassed to be naked, but that was only half the truth. "Cain, where is your brother?" "How should I know?" Now that wasn't a lie. "Am I my brother's keeper?" That wasn't a lie, just a question. But can you see how the devil infected our human race, and since then we have never had to teach any child to lie, but it has been a constant struggle for our parents to teach us to speak the truth, the whole truth, and nothing but the truth.

So it goes right the way down. The devil's name in Greek is *diabolos*, which means "slanderer". One day there was a good man on earth, a man who loved God, called Job. The devil went to God himself and said, "God, that man doesn't love you for your own sake. He only loves you because you have given him a good job, a lovely family, health, and strength. You take those things away and mark my words he's a crooked man at heart."

God said, "Satan you're lying. You take away his health, take away his family, take away his business, and see what he's like."

The devil is always imputing ulterior motives, always slandering men of God.

One day there came into this sad, sick world of lies, this world that the devil controlled (so the truth is at a premium), for the first time, a man who told the truth, the whole truth, and nothing but the truth. His name was Jesus, and he said, "I am the truth". When he came into this sick world, the truth confronted all the lies. There is never any trace of flattery in anything Jesus said about others. Nor is there any trace of falsehood in anything he said about people. If he called a man a "fox", which he did, that man was a fox. If he called a man or a woman a precious person, then they were precious. Everything he said about other people was true. It lost him many friends but it was the truth, the whole truth, and nothing but the truth. He could look into a man's life and describe that life inside out, and it was always true. He never made a mistake, never bore false witness to anybody else. Nor did he bear false witness to himself, even through modesty. He made amazing claims for himself but they were the truth, the whole truth, and nothing but the truth. What happened to this man at the age of thirty-three, this man who was the Son of God – God, who is truth therefore his Son is truth? The truth lived among us and lived in a world of lies. What was going to happen? You know. There was going to be a direct confrontation between truth and falsehood and it came at the trial of Jesus. If ever there was injustice it was there. There has never been such a case of miscarried justice as at the trial of him who was the Truth.

They tried to get false witnesses. They couldn't get the witnesses to agree, but far from charging the witnesses with perjury and throwing them into prison as they deserved (in fact the law said that they should die because they were trying to perjure a man to death), they continued with the trial. Finally, a witness was found who said: "This man said, 'Destroy this temple made with hands and I will raise it again in three days, a temple made without hands.'"

You know there was only one misquotation in that whole sentence, but it was enough to make the high priest ask Jesus a leading question. He said, "I adjure you, tell us, are you the Son of the living God?"

Jesus replied with the truth, the whole truth, and nothing but the truth. He said, "I am, and you will see the Son of Man coming in the clouds of heaven." It was the truth, and they condemned him to death for speaking the truth.

Jesus died for not speaking the truth in their eyes. "Blasphemy", they said – that can't be true; you can't be the Son of God.

I think the worst thing of all, the climax of it all, was that even his best friend told lies about him that night. Can you see that the devil threw everything at Jesus? The devil got hold of everyone he could to tell lies that night. Simon Peter said, "I don't know who you're talking about. I have nothing to do with him." Lies, lies, lies. He who was the truth went out to die.

If there is no God of truth, that would have been the end of it. If there is no God in heaven who is concerned about truth on earth, then Jesus would be like John Brown mouldering in his grave right now. But there is a God of truth and glory, a God who will not let lies conquer truth. The God of truth raised from the dead on the third day him who was the truth. From that Easter Sunday morning we know for ever that truth is more powerful than lies, and that Jesus is more powerful than Satan. Therefore, we can bring him these soiled lives of ours that have broken this commandment and we can say, "Jesus, would you repeat that victory in me?"

It is the only way we will manage it. You just try to stop

gossiping in your own strength! Try and control what you say yourself – you never will. The New Testament is very realistic in this matter. It virtually admits that it will be a great battle. It may well be the very last thing that God gets under his complete control. James, the Lord's own brother, wrote, "When you've got your tongue under control you'll be perfect." The glory of it is that the God who begins a good work in us will continue it until it is complete. He will perfect us. He is determined to. He will go on struggling with us, chastising us, humbling us, loving us, and helping us, until he gets this battle won, because truth must conquer. As a boy I was constantly reminded of this by a brass plate above our dining-room fireplace, which read: "VINCIT VERITAS".

The glorious thing is that he not only has in mind enabling you by his strength to stop bearing false witness *to* others, he also will enable you to bear false witness *from* others. For everyone who stands for the truth in this world of ours will have lies spread about them. You cannot avoid that. It happened to Jesus and it will happen to you. That is why in the Sermon on the Mount he said, "Blessed are you when men shall say all manner of evil against you falsely for my sake." It shows you belong to the kingdom of heaven and you follow a noble army of prophets. Blessed are you.

Here then is the meaning of the ninth commandment: truth. James, the Lord's brother, said more than any other apostle about the damage that can be done by the tongue. In Mark chapter 3 we read that the family of Jesus "went to take charge of him" because it was said that, "He is out of his mind".

All of us have things we have said that we regret bitterly and deeply. When Jesus died, he died to set us free from the penalty of our sin and from the power of it too. Praise God!

10

Do Not Covet

Here is one of the worst cases of coveting in the Bible. It is the account of a king who wanted something he hadn't got.

Naboth, a man from Jezreel, had a vineyard on the outskirts of the city near King Ahab's palace, and one day the king talked to him about selling him this land. "I want it for a garden," the king explained, "because it's so convenient to the palace." He offered cash or, if Naboth preferred, a piece of better land in exchange.

But Naboth replied, "Not on your life; that land has been in my family for generations."

So Ahab went back to the palace angry and sullen. He refused to eat and went to bed with his face to the wall. [Fancy a king doing that.] "What in the world is the matter?" his wife Jezebel asked him. "Why aren't you eating? What has made you so upset and angry?"

"I asked Naboth to sell me his vineyard or to trade it and he refused," Ahab told her.

"Are you the king of Israel or not?" Jezebel demanded. "Get up and eat and don't worry about it. I'll get you Naboth's vineyard."

So she wrote letters in Ahab's name, sealed them with his seal, and addressed them to the civic leaders of Jezreel where Naboth lived. In her letter, she commanded, "Call the citizens together for fasting and prayer. Then summon Naboth and find two scoundrels who will accuse him of cursing God and the king, and then take him out and execute him." The city fathers followed the queen's instructions. They called the meeting, put

Naboth on trial, and then two men, who had no conscience, accused him of cursing God and the king, and he was dragged outside the city and stoned to death. The city officials then sent word to Jezebel that Naboth was dead. When Jezebel heard the news she said to Ahab, "You know the vineyard Naboth wouldn't sell you? Well you can have it now. He's dead."

So Ahab went down to the vineyard to claim it, but the Lord said to Elijah, "Go to Samaria to meet King Ahab. He will be at Naboth's vineyard, taking possession of it, and give him this message from me, 'Isn't killing Naboth bad enough, must you rob him too? Because you have done this, dogs shall lick your blood outside the city just as they licked the blood of Naboth.'"

"So my enemy has found me," Ahab exclaimed to Elijah.

"Yes," Elijah answered, "I have come to place God's curse upon you because you have sold yourself to the devil. The Lord is going to bring great harm to you and sweep you away. He will not let a single one of your male descendants survive. He is going to destroy your family as he did the family of King Jeroboam and the family of King Baasha, for you made him very angry and have led all of Israel into sin. The Lord also told me that the dogs of Jezreel shall tear apart the body of your wife, Jezebel. The members of your family who die in the city shall be eaten by dogs, and those who die in the country shall be eaten by vultures."

1 Kings 21:1–24

No one else was so completely sold out to the devil as Ahab, for his wife Jezebel encouraged him to do every sort of evil. That was the most expensive piece of land he ever bought. It cost him everything—his life, his throne, his family, his wife, the lot, and all because he wanted a man's back garden, one of his neighbours.

The passage which follows is entitled *"I Want."*

"If only.... I want to be able to do what I like. If only I was finished with school. I want to get away from here. If only I was older. I want to get around a bit before I settle down. If only my parents would leave me alone. I want to be popular.

DO NOT COVET

If only I had a car. I want to be left alone. If only I had plenty of money. I want to be famous. If only I could get a better job. I want to live it up before I'm old. If only people would leave me alone. I want to get married. If only I could afford better clothes. I want a better life. If only there was something to do. I want; I don't know what I want. If only.... I want—I want."

That was written by a young person, and one of the strange laws of human nature is that the more we have, the more we want. Strange that we go on believing this fiction, for it is a fiction—that if only we could have that, then we would be satisfied. If only we could reach this goal, if only we could possess that, if only we could be like so and so – then we would finally be happy. Yet on the whole it is affluent nations that are the most acquisitive, and the more we have, the more we want. This country has so much compared with two-thirds of the world's population, yet most elections here are won on one issue: the money in your pocket, increased prosperity, more goods. But I am not going to teach here about the political or social scene because the tenth commandment is primarily directed not to rich nations as opposed to poor ones, but to the individual. In the commandment the word "you" is in the singular. But I have mentioned the general matter of poverty and wealth because coveting is seen in its more horrible nature when you realise we ought to be among the most thankful people in the whole world. We ought to be thoroughly content with what we have. Somebody has said that if all the world were invited to put their troubles in one big heap, and each person invited to take a fair share back, we would rather go back to our original state.

We are concerned in the tenth commandment with something very simple: greed. It is the only one of the ten commandments that is concerned with inward thoughts and feelings rather than with outward acts or words; it's the one that goes right to our hearts, and it is the only one of the ten that Saul of Tarsus failed to keep as a devout Jew. He said that, as touching the law, as far as outward appearance went, he was blameless. He was a Hebrew of the Hebrews, a Pharisee of the Pharisees. Nobody could fault him on the law for the simple reason that nobody could see inside his heart. But in his moments of self-admission, in Romans chapter seven, he says that as a Pharisee there was one law he could not keep: "You shall not covet." The Pharisees were pretty notorious for this, too. Nobody knows if you are greedy in your heart for what someone else has.

When I look through the Bible, I find that man after man and woman after woman was ruined by this one thing. Here is a quick list I made. In the Old Testament I began with a woman: Eve. She saw something that she shouldn't have, and she wanted it, and so it wasn't long before she took it. The next person I noted was a man: Lot. When Abraham and Lot looked at the Promised Land, Abraham, who was the older man, the uncle, said to his nephew, "Which part of the country do you want?" Lot looked down to the Jordan Valley and it was prosperous and fertile, and he said, "I'll have that," and he went to live in a place called Sodom, next door to another place called Gomorrah – and it nearly ruined Lot.

The next person was a man who brought a whole nation to within an inch of disaster because he alone saw something that belonged to someone else and wanted it. His name was Achan. You can read the story in the book of Joshua when the Israelites, having defeated Jericho, went on to take the city of Ai. They did not know that one man among them had seen something in Jericho and taken it because he coveted it. They failed to take the city of Ai because God knew about Achan. I put down the sons of Eli, the priest who trained Samuel as a boy. Eli's sons wrecked their father's ministry and forfeited their own because they coveted and were greedy. Then there were Samuel's own sons, who suffered from the same fault. Then Saul, the first king of Israel. I noticed Ahab. Then the servant of the prophet Elisha, a man called Gehazi, who wasn't going to let Naaman get healed for nothing and wanted something for it. You find again and again, throughout the pages of the Bible, men and women ruined by greed.

When we turn to the New Testament, the situation doesn't alter. The first man noted here was Judas. We often say that he sold his Saviour for thirty pieces of silver. He didn't, he sold himself for thirty pieces of silver. He sold his life; he didn't live another twenty-four hours. There was Simon Magus, the man who saw Simon Peter laying hands on folk and they received power; the Holy Ghost came on them. Simon Magus pulled out his wallet and said, "How much for the secret of the trick? I'm a magician too and I'd like your trick; I'd like your secret."

Peter said, "To hell with you and your money. You repent of this thing."

Ananias and Sapphira – I suppose you could say, from one point of view, they were the first Christian "martyrs", but they were martyrs to possessions, not for the faith. Demetrius is one of the saddest figures in the whole Bible and there's only a sentence about him: "Demetrius was a man who found that greed was too much for him." So I could go on: Felix was another, Demas was another. The pages of holy writ are full of men and women whose lives were ruined by greed—just that.

The Bible links greed very closely to the eyes. Sight is a gift, but in some people it stimulates greed. Eve saw the fruit on the tree, desired it and took it. Achan saw a beautiful ornament that he wanted and he took it. We have to walk through a world today, in which the advertisers are telling us to want, want and want again. It is very difficult when you can't even watch a programme on the television without it being interrupted with someone saying, "Everybody else has this, millions of others have this – why don't you have it?" We live in a pressurised world, in which greed is being encouraged for commercial reasons. It's not easy to be content with what you have when you see what others have.

One of the most profoundly disturbing influences in the whole world is the spread of entertainment media. People working in poorer regions of the world have told me that what has caused deep resentment, anger, discontent and determination to have more is the fact that Hollywood has exported films to them which have shown a standard of living and a way of life in lush apartments that these people never dreamt of until the mass media came to their country. I am not saying that we should have left them in their poverty. What I am saying is that we have flaunted a way of life that was a million miles beyond theirs.

Now greed has a second cousin called "pride". The two often go together. We are greedy because we are proud. I want to refer to three common habits which reveal our greed. The first is the habit of collecting things. I am not saying it is a wrong habit; I am saying, however, that the habit of collecting things carries with it a terrible temptation. What is your collection? Stamps? Antiques?

I remember going to lunch with a man at whose church I had preached one Sunday. He said, "I'd like to show you my collection afterwards. I spent many years collecting it." He kept me in the dark; he wouldn't tell me what it was. After lunch he took me round the corner of the house and there was a huge hangar of a shed. He flung wide the doors and inside were about twenty-five stagecoaches, all kept locked up there. He must have spent a fortune on them, all beautifully renovated. There they were: "My stagecoaches, my collection." Now if you are given to collecting anything, there are two questions you need to ask: what is my collection doing to me, and what can it do for someone else?

There is some need for collecting – preserving that which is valuable from the past. There is need for those who will collect things that are going to be of help to other people. But if my collection is simply making me more proud or more greedy, simply making me want more and more of this thing so that I can say "I've got more", then we have become possessed by our possessions. If, on the other hand, I am doing it so that I may preserve for others and share with them something that is of interest and value to them, than it is a very different matter. I mention it because it is a common habit. Most of us collect something.

Secondly, there is the habit of bargaining. All the world loves a bargain. "Do you know how much I got it for?" We have to watch that in our bargaining we are not feeding this thing called greed. Sometimes we love a bargain because we got it for less than its value. It is in my blood. It was in my grandfather's blood, and my grandmother used to spend the days of his retirement sending him back to the auction rooms with useless junk. But he would say, "Look, I got this lovely big picture for just ten shillings."

"Take it back," said my grandmother – or there wouldn't have been room in the house for her!

I saw a lovely little cartoon in a magazine. It showed a shop window full of fur coats, slashing reductions: fifty percent off. There was a lady looking in, and a meek little husband was standing by her side, muttering to himself, "I could tell her how to save 100%." We need to ask: am I buying something I don't want and don't need because it appeals to my greed to get it at that price?

The third, very common habit which has swept through our country and which is rotting the moral guts of the nation, is the habit of gambling, mentioned earlier. There are many forms of it, some very subtle. We had the wool pulled over our eyes when premium bonds were introduced. It was said that it wasn't a gamble. What is it? You are gambling the interest, not the capital. That was the first time, for a very long time, that our nation officially introduced gambling to our economic life. But it is now such a national disease, and many spend far more on gambling than on food.

I once went to visit a dying man and I'll never forget it. He lay in his bed coughing his life away. Do you know what he was doing in his last few hours, when he should have been preparing to meet his Maker? He was filling in a football pool. I asked, "What are you doing that for at this time?"

He replied, "Because I made no other provision for my family and I'm staking everything on this."

It is a habit that panders to greed, and a gambler makes a poor employer. He's trying to get something for nothing and to get rich quickly.

What is wrong with greed? What is wrong with wanting what somebody else has? Why not? They've got it, why shouldn't I want it?

First, it is a sin that can drag a man to hell, but I don't believe that God ever calls a thing a sin for any arbitrary reason. He doesn't just say, "I think I'll call that a sin because they seem to be enjoying it." He doesn't think like that. When God calls a thing a sin, he does it because it's bad for us – and because he made us, he knows what is best. He knows in the long term what greed does to a person – he knows that it will destroy them.

There are three things the Bible says about greed – coveting. First, that a man's heart is drugged. Second, that a man's mind is deceived. Third, that a man's soul is destroyed.

First of all, a man's heart is *drugged*. The extraordinary thing is that the more he has, the more he will want. He will never be satisfied. He will always be dreaming of a bigger business; he will always be pulling down his barns and building greater ones.

I remember hearing of a cattle dealer who was so busy making money on cattle that finally he had a breakdown, and his doctor sent him away to the southwest of England to get a complete rest, a break to recover. When he got there, he had his first meal in the hotel and, after the meal, made straight for the reception desk and said to the receptionist, "Do you know of any farmers around here who might have some cattle to sell?" He just couldn't get away from it. A man's heart is drugged. He becomes obsessed with his wants rather than his needs.

The second thing is that a man's mind is *deceived* in two particulars. One thing is that he is deceived into thinking he is successful when he has got a lot. We even use the phrase of a man who has made a lot of money: "He's done well." But has he? You could be very deceived in that. The other deception is that a man is not only deceived in his mind as to his success, but he is deceived as to his security. "Take your ease. You've done well. You've built up a business. You've filled your barns. Take your ease now and retire and enjoy it." But God says, "You fool, you won't enjoy it because tonight you're going to leave it behind. Tonight your soul is required of you."

Thirdly, a man's soul is *destroyed*. Jesus says, in one of his matchless stories, that the seed of God's Word can be planted in someone's life, seed that could germinate and produce life, and it gets choked with weeds. What are those weeds? You study Jesus' own interpretation of the parable of the sower: the deceitfulness of riches chokes. A man who could have been saved is choked and the seed never germinates and the spiritual life never comes and he has killed his soul. What profit does a man make if he can say, "I own the world; I've taken over every business I can in my line. It's now a worldwide concern." What profit has he made if he loses his own life?

What is the cure? Here are four steps. The first is *conversion*. It is very difficult to get converted if you are rich. By Bible standards, most people in our society are rich. Jesus said that it is hard for a rich man. It is easier to get a camel through the eye of a needle than to get a rich man into glory. That is one of the reasons why it is so difficult to get people converted in England today – because we are rich. We ride around in our cars. We don't need anything. We *want* a lot of things, but most of us don't *need* anything.

So we are rich and Jesus said it is hard, but there is no hope for a man until he is converted—the first step. There was one wealthy young man who came to Jesus. It is one of the saddest incidents recorded. He came to Jesus, who told him how to live forever, and he knew it was right. He turned away sadly, and Jesus let him go because he had too much greed. It still held his heart. Conversion means changing from the prodigal son, who said "Give me" to the prodigal son who said "Forgive me."

The second step is *consecration* – having been forgiven, to give yourself and your possessions to God. A visiting preacher spoke of how he did this. He listed everything that he possessed. He was astonished. He didn't think he had a lot, but he filled quite a few foolscap sheets. Have you ever written down everything you possess? You will be shattered as to how much you have. Then he went through the list and said, "Lord, I'm going to give each of these things to you, and you tell me what I can keep and what you want me to get rid of," and he went through the list. "My camera?"

The Lord said, "You can keep that. I can use that." So he ticked it.

"My records?"

"No, you can get rid of those" – so he put a cross.

He went through each thing so that even the things he kept he had given away. Do you understand? It is what consecration means. So you don't talk about "my house" or "my car" any more. It is *his* business, *his* car, and *his* house.

The third step is to learn *contentment*. It is one of the hardest lessons in life and it takes many years for some people to learn. But there was Paul, a man who could say, "I am content with a lot or a little." That is the great secret. What a lesson! God wants some people to have a lot because they can use it for him, and he leaves others with little. Yet those who have really learned that the Lord is their Shepherd say, "I shall not want. I have learned to be content with much or with little." I don't know which is the more difficult lesson to learn – I suspect learning to be content with a lot when other things are within your reach.

The fourth step is to learn to *redirect your covetousness* in the right direction. Do you know where in the New Testament Christians are told to covet? The right kind of coveting is the answer to the wrong kind. *Coveting* is wanting something that somebody else has – to want it for yourself. You are not to covet your neighbour's house, wife, donkey, servant—anything. Isn't that an interesting order? House first, wife second, donkey third, but anyway, you are not to covet anything that is his except one thing. The Bible says: "Covet earnestly the spiritual gifts."

Why? Because those gifts, when you read about them, are gifts that would enable you to serve other people – so you are coveting something that will help you to help them.

That is what we are to covet. We are to covet ministries to other people. We are to covet gifts of the Spirit so that we can share with others the riches of Christ. We are to covet that which will enable us to *give*, not to get – not to covet gifts that will enable us to make a lot of money. Oh, what gifts there are to covet!

In summary, here are the four steps: *conversion* (get right with God; "forgive me"); *consecration* ("Lord, it's not just me that you have now, but you've bought me, my clothes, my house, my job; you've bought the lot; here it is—everything"); and learning to *be content* with whatever the Lord gives you back – he may give you a lot or he may give you a little, but be content; *covet those things that will enable you to go out into a needy world and give people what they need.*

Do you realise that the Lord Jesus never owned a house – he had nowhere to lay his head; he finished up with nothing, for even his clothes were taken from him and gambled over – yet he was content. He had everything he needed, but he had more. He had everything that everybody else needed, and he gave it to them. He was rich, yet for our sakes became poor, that we through his poverty might become rich. He came into the world in a dirty stable and there was not even a cot or a pram to put him in. He had nothing to leave when he left the world except his peace, but his riches are yours if you believe.

Printed in Great Britain
by Amazon